EASY PIANO

Arranged by Bill Boyd

Walt Disney PICTURES
PRESENTS

Beauty and the Beast

Artwork © The Walt Disney Company

ISBN 0-7935-1293-X

7777 West Bluemound Road P.O. Box 13819 Milwaukee, WI 53213

Beauty and the Beast

BELLE

Lyrics by HOWARD ASHMAN
Music by ALAN MENKEN

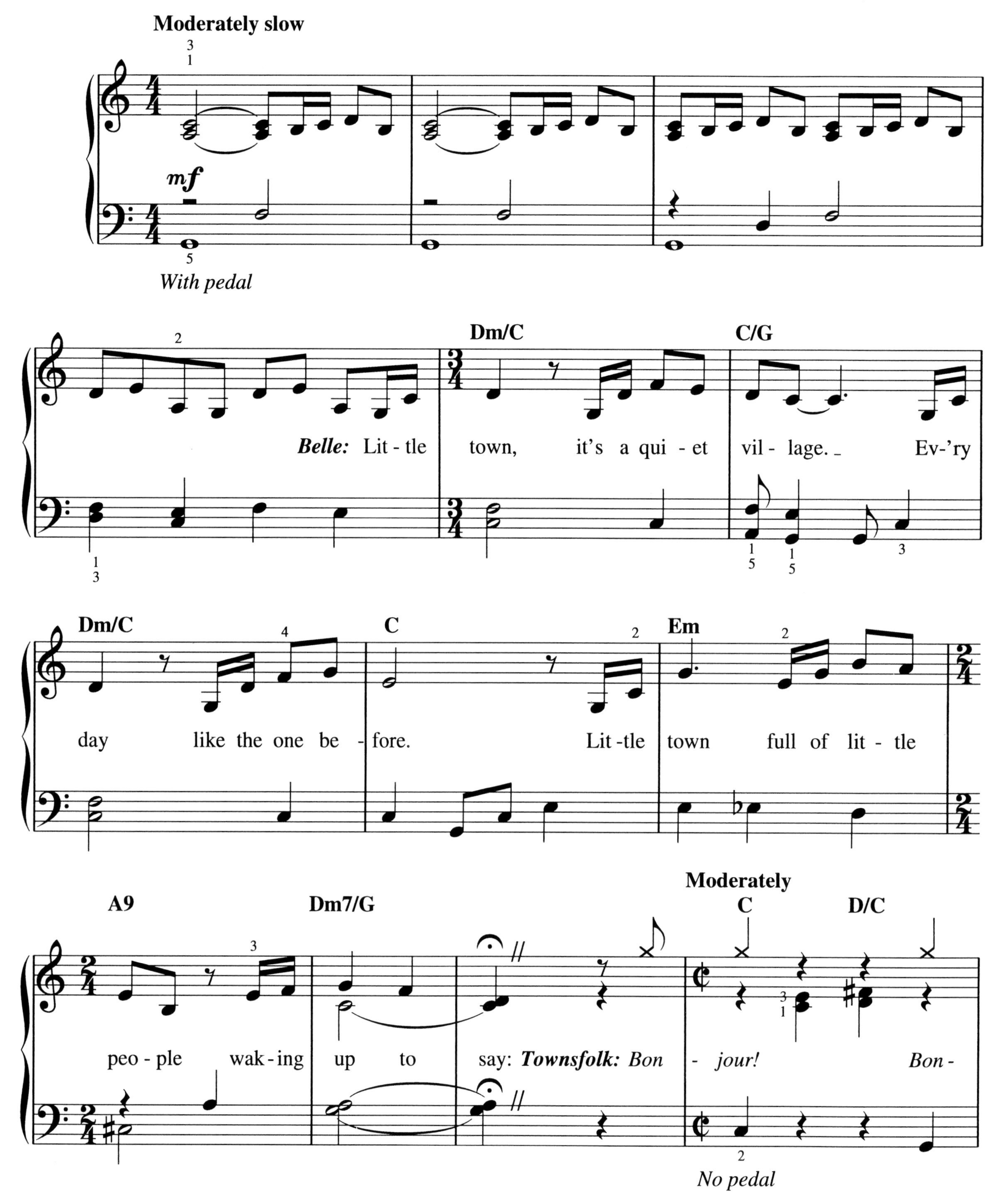

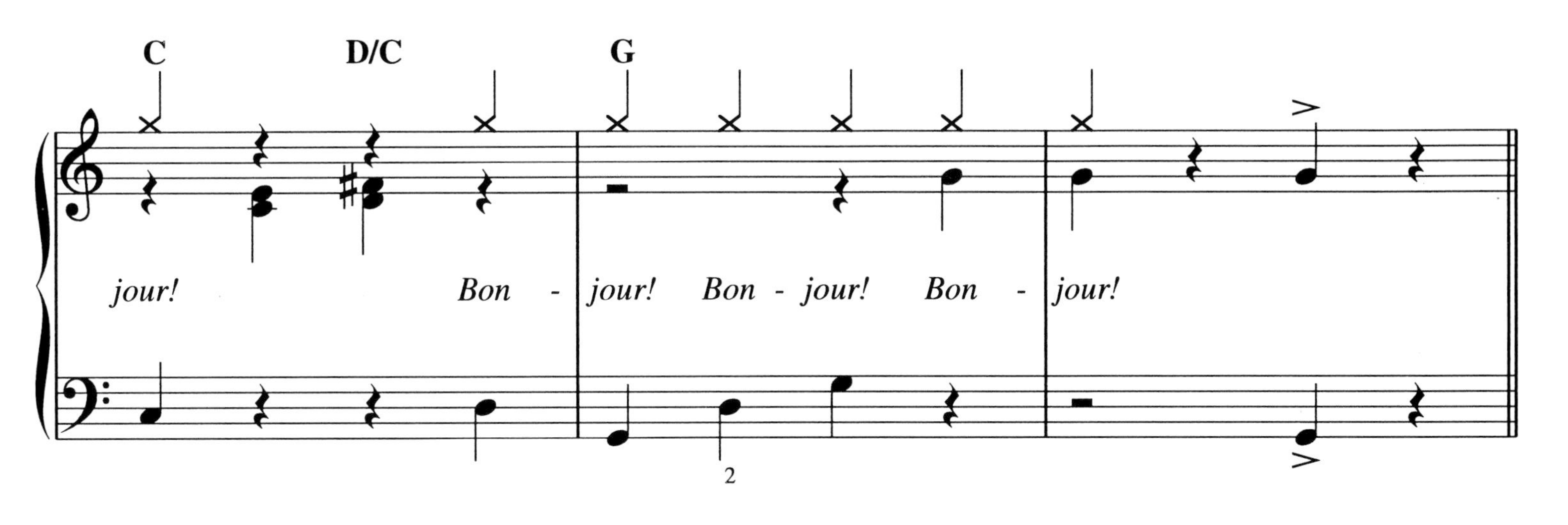
C D/C G
jour! Bon - jour! Bon - jour! Bon - jour!

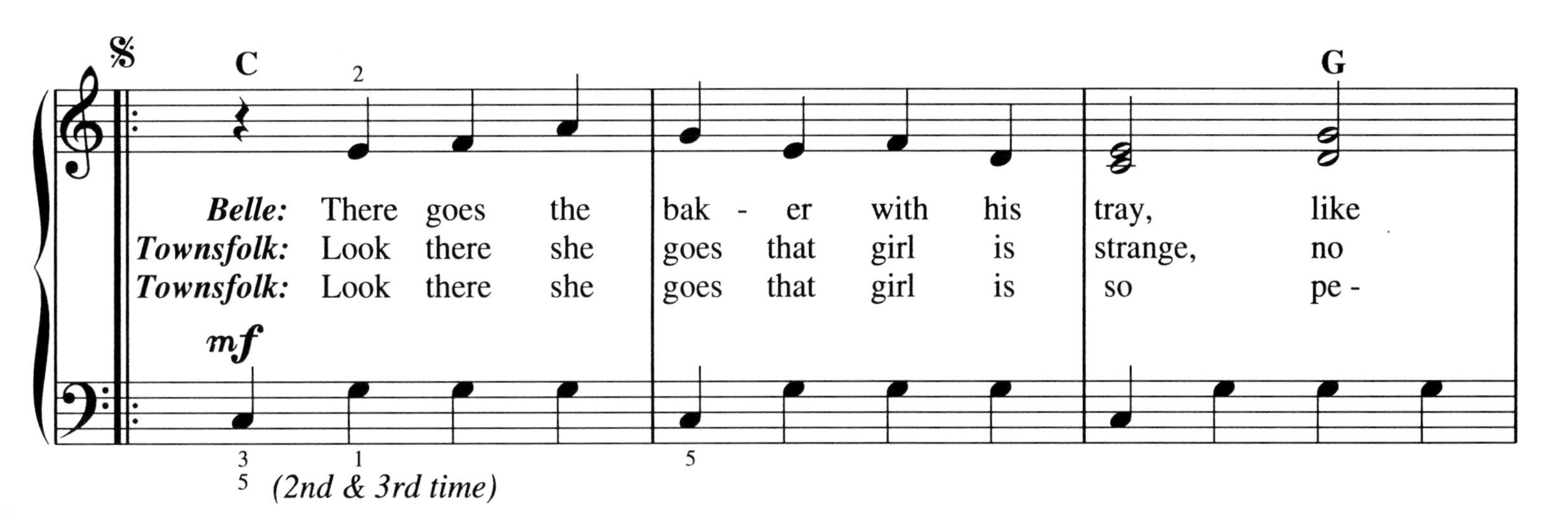
C G
Belle: There goes the bak - er with his tray, like
Townsfolk: Look there she goes that girl is strange, no
Townsfolk: Look there she goes that girl is so pe -
mf
(2nd & 3rd time)

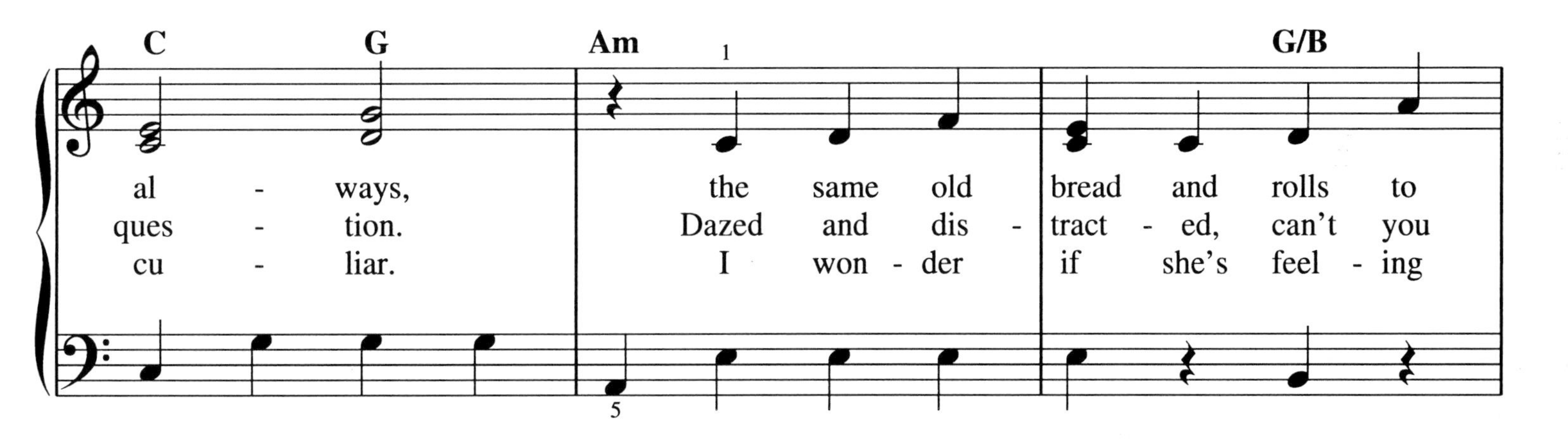
C G Am G/B
al - ways, the same old bread and rolls to
ques - tion. Dazed and dis - tract - ed, can't you
cu - liar. I won - der if she's feel - ing

C E♭ F
sell. Ev - 'ry morn - ing just the
tell? Nev - er part of an - y
well. With a dream - y, far - off

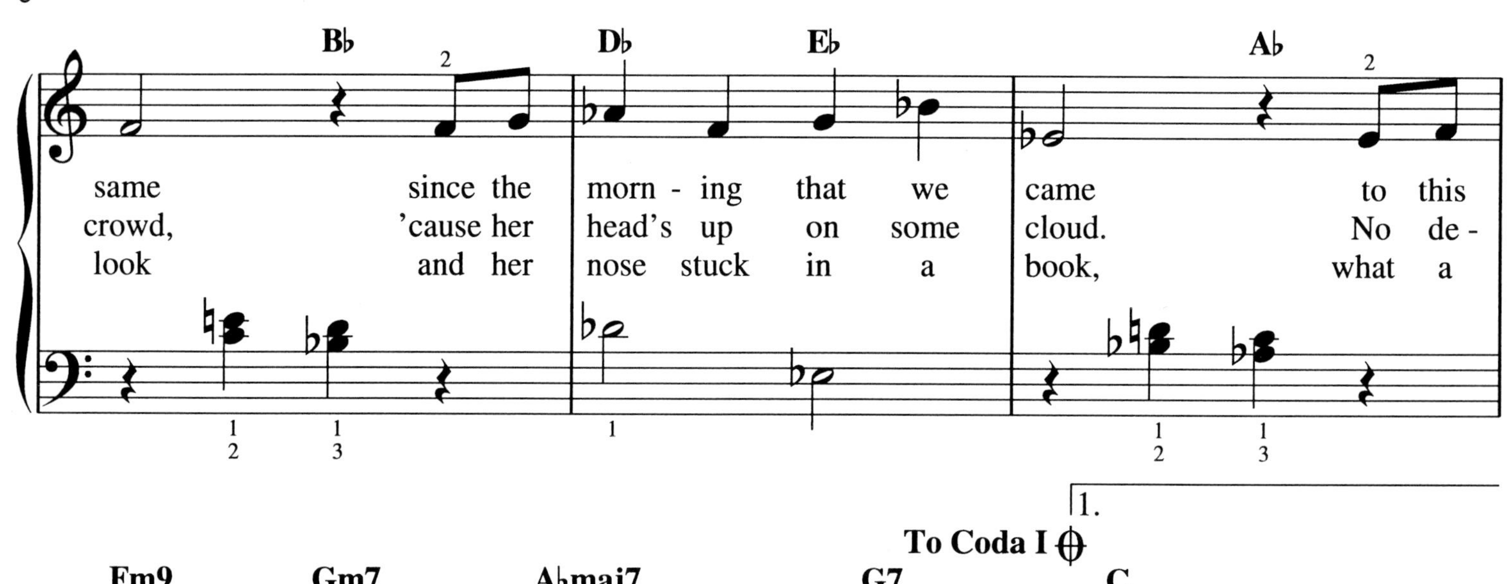
B♭
D♭
E♭
A♭
same since the morn - ing that we came to this
crowd, 'cause her head's up on some cloud. No de -
look and her nose stuck in a book, what a

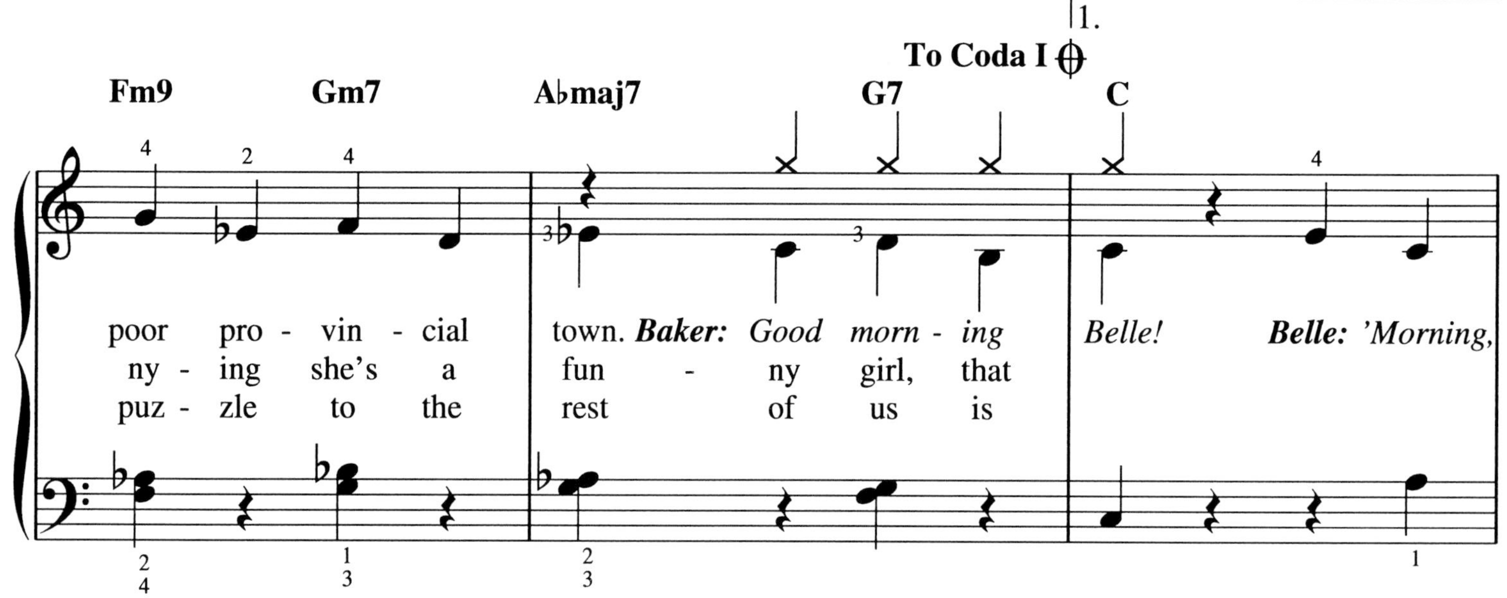
1.
To Coda I
Fm9
Gm7
A♭maj7
G7
C
poor pro - vin - cial town. Baker: Good morn - ing Belle! Belle: 'Morning,
ny - ing she's a fun - ny girl, that
puz - zle to the rest of us is

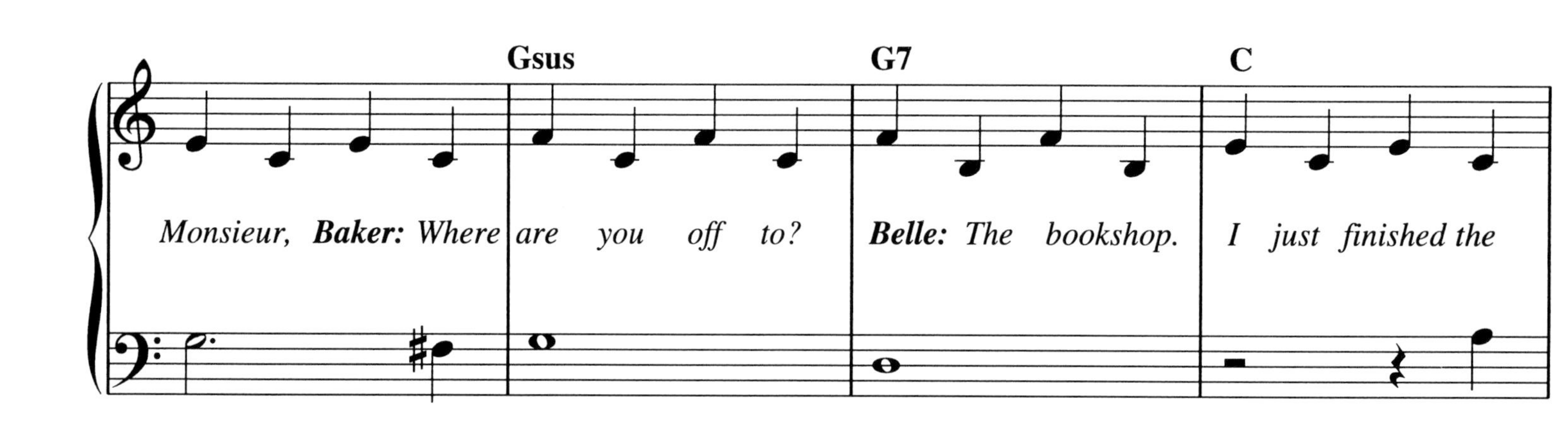
Gsus
G7
C
Monsieur, Baker: Where are you off to? Belle: The bookshop. I just finished the

Gsus
G7
Cadd9
most wonderful story about a beanstalk and an ogre and a... Baker: That's nice. Ma -

2.
C
rie! The baguettes! Hurry up!
Belle.

F G F G F G/F
Man I: Bon-jour.
Woman I: Good day.
Man I: How is your

C/E F G F G F G7/F
fam - 'ly?
Woman II: Bon- jour.
Man II: Good day.
Woman II: How is your

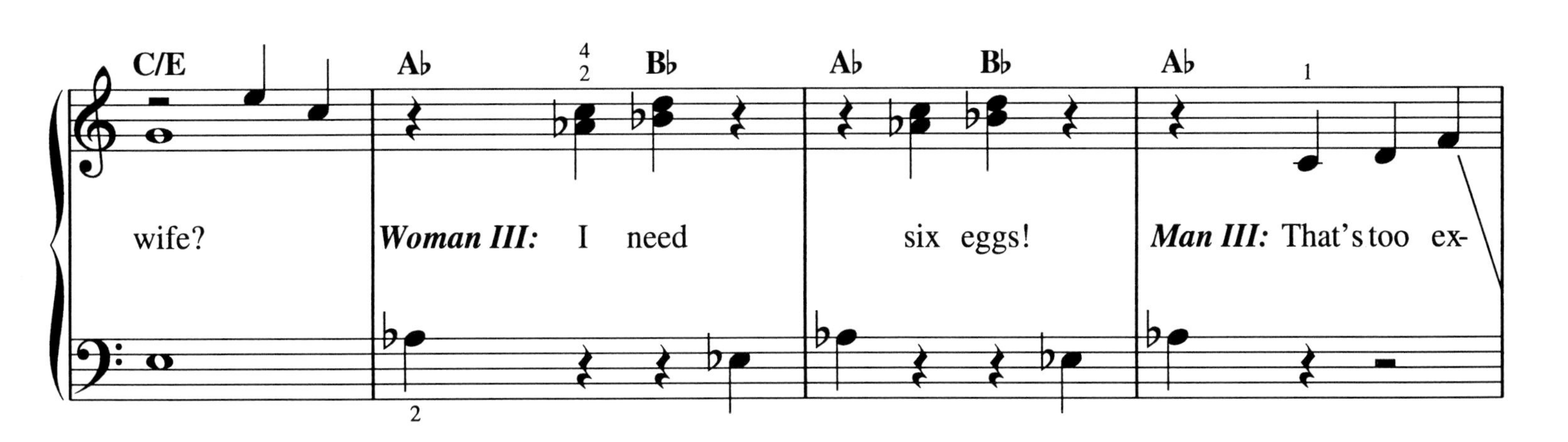
C/E A♭ B♭ A♭ B♭ A♭
wife?
Woman III: I need six eggs!
Man III: That's too ex-

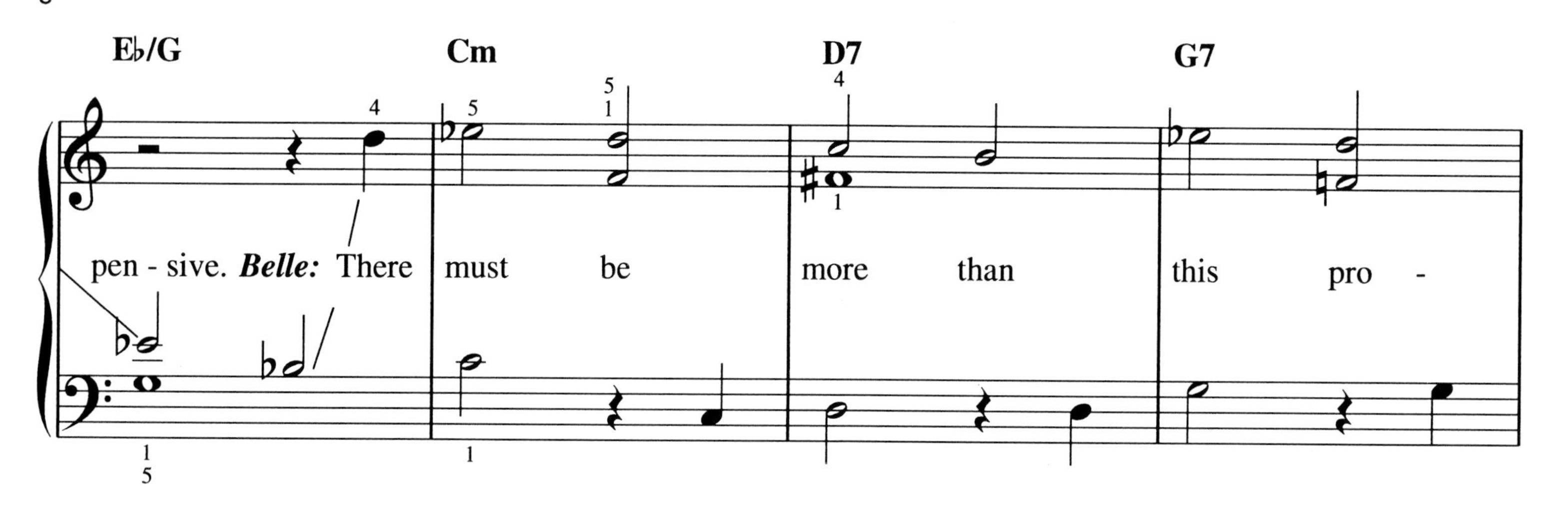
Eb/G
Cm
D7
G7
pen - sive. Belle: There
must be
more than
this pro -

C
(2) Second time
Gsus
vin - cial
life. Bookseller:
anything new? Bookseller:
mp
Ah, Belle!
Ha, ha! Not since
Belle: Good morning.
yesterday.

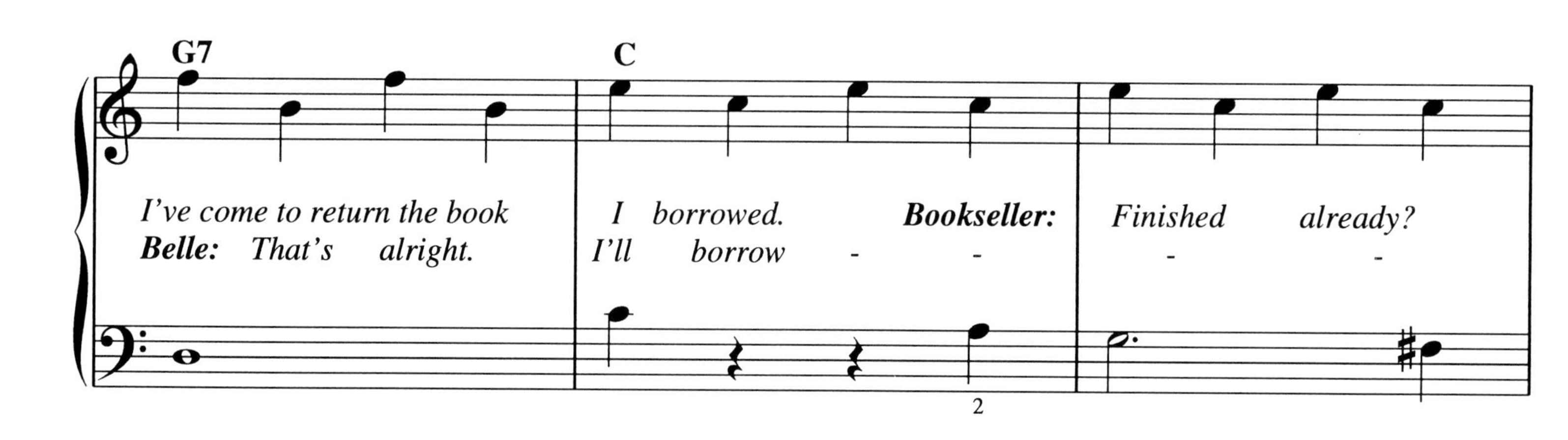
G7
C
I've come to return the book
Belle: That's alright.
I borrowed. Bookseller:
I'll borrow
Finished already?

Gsus
G7
Eb
Belle: Oh, I couldn't put it
this one! Bookseller:
down. Have you got
That one? But you've
read it twice!
daring sword fights,
Belle: Well, it's my
magic

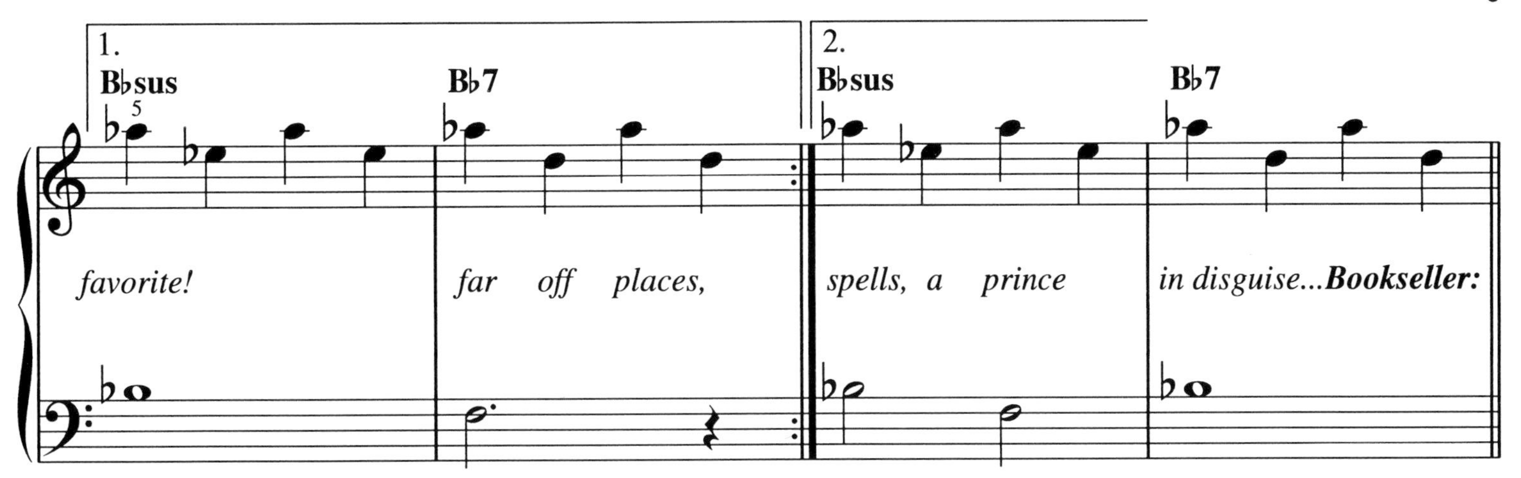
1.
B♭sus
B♭7
2.
B♭sus
B♭7
favorite!
far off places,
spells, a prince
in disguise... Bookseller:

C
1.
Gsus
If you like it all that
much, it's
yours! Belle: But
insist. Belle: Well, thank you.

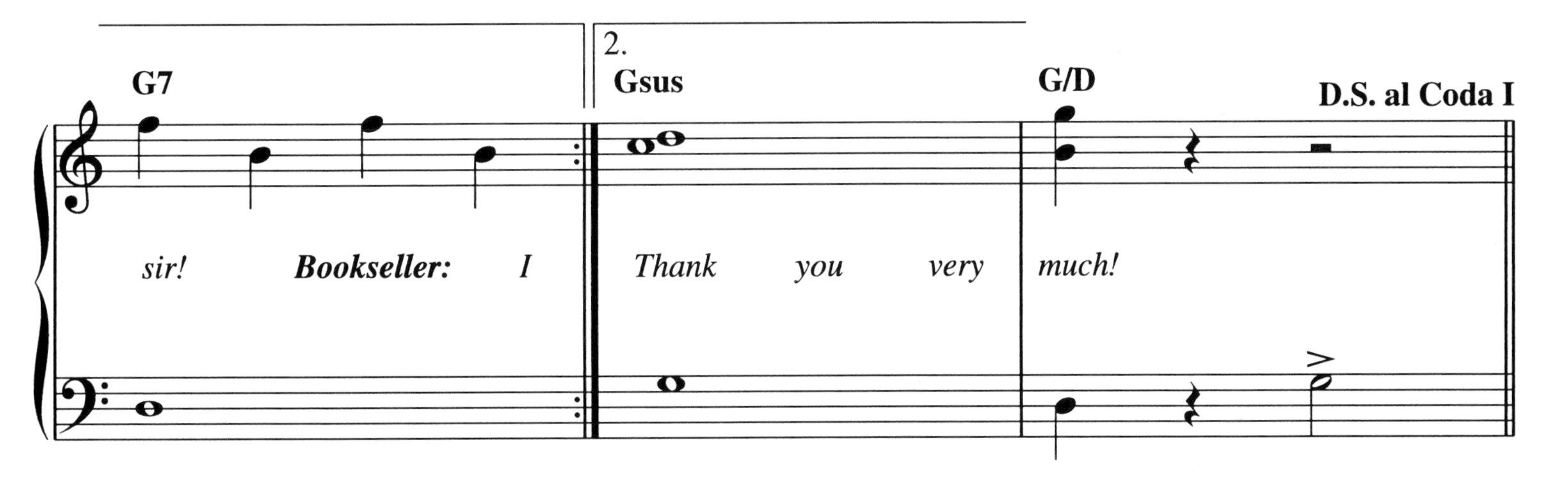
G7
2.
Gsus
G/D
D.S. al Coda I
sir! Bookseller: I
Thank you very
much!

CODA I
C
F
Belle.
Belle:
Oh,
With pedal

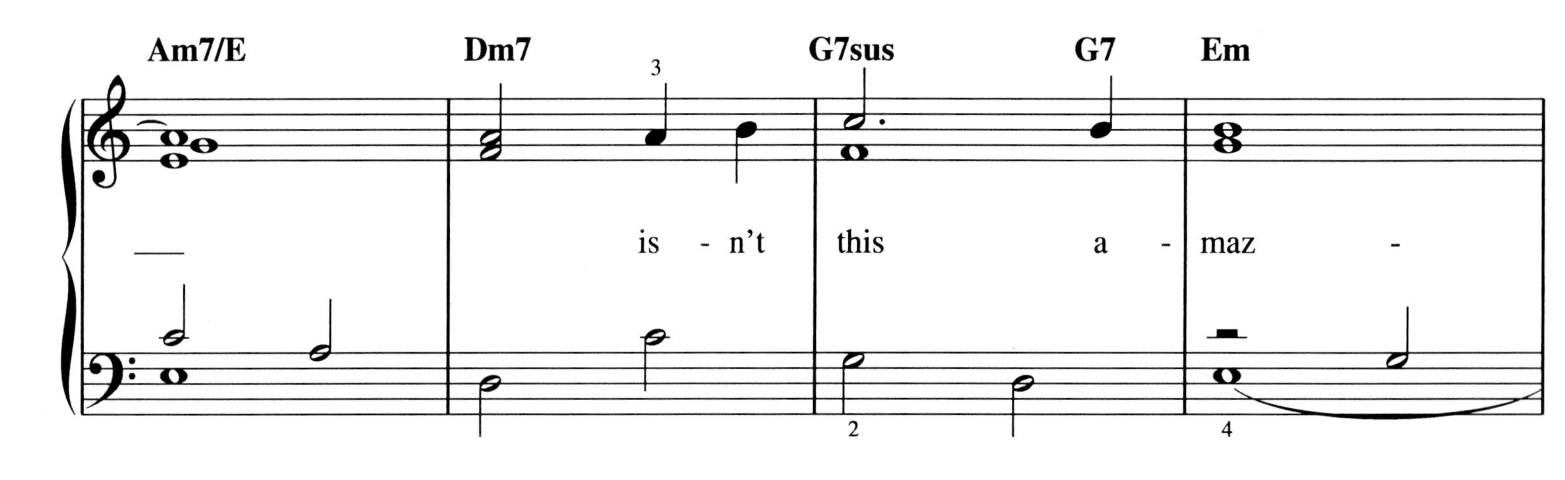
Am7/E
Dm7
G7sus
G7
Em
is - n't this a - maz -

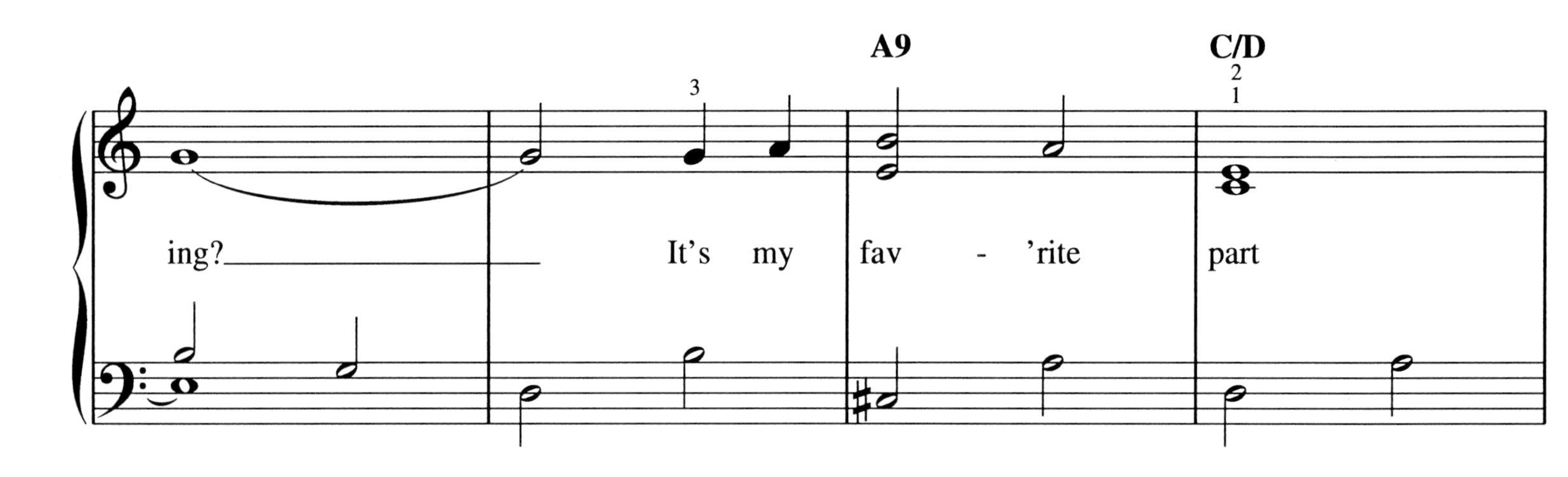
A9
C/D
ing? It's my fav - 'rite part

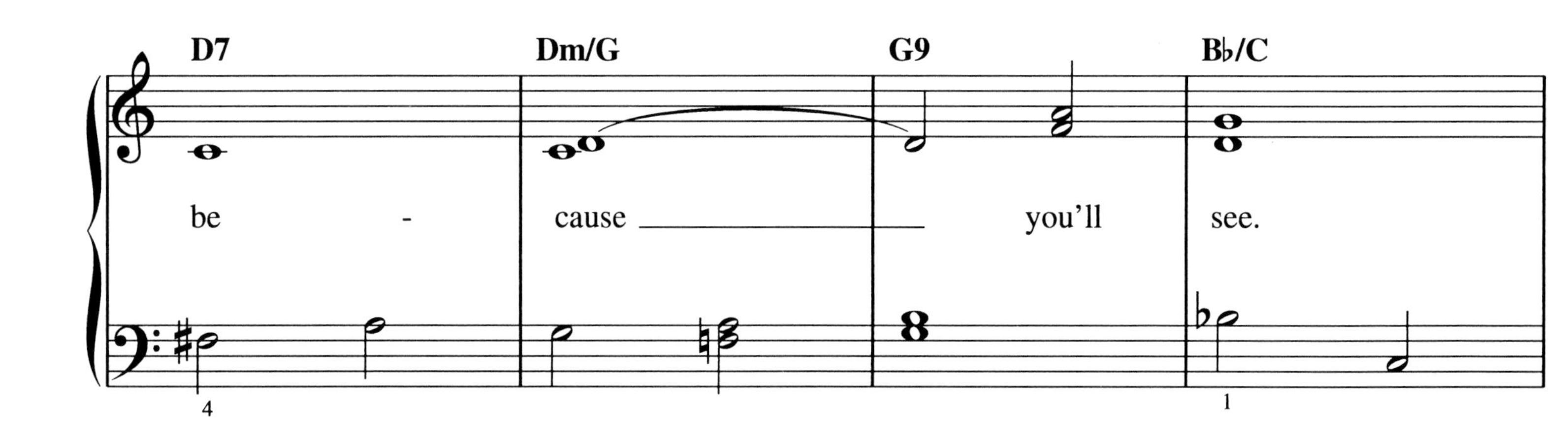
D7
Dm/G
G9
B♭/C
be - cause you'll see.

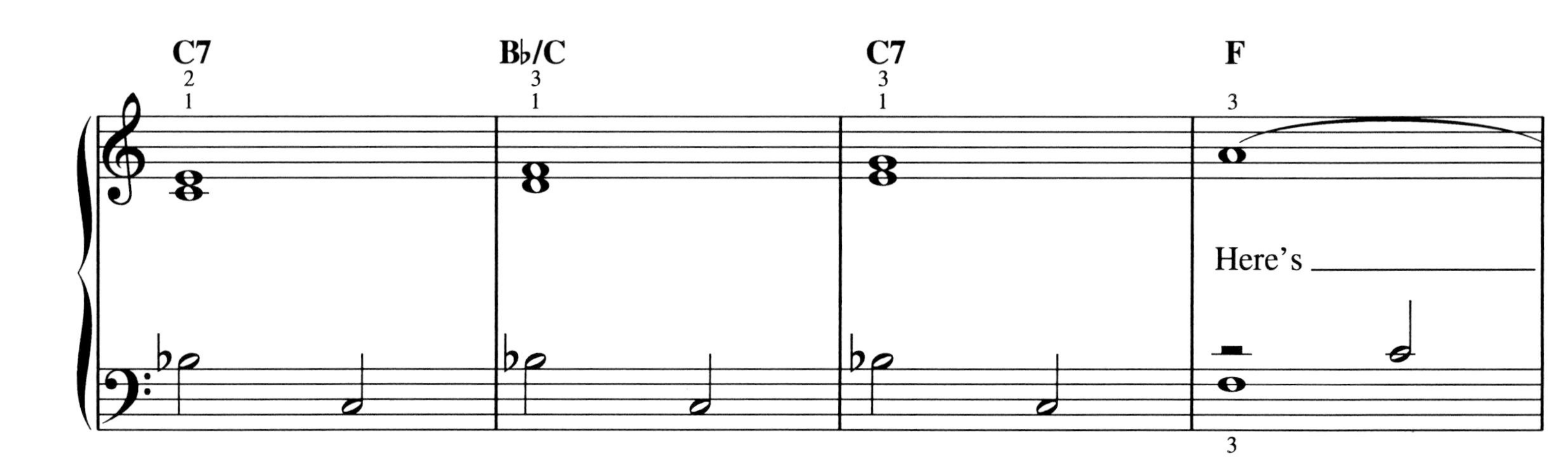
C7
B♭/C
C7
F
Here's

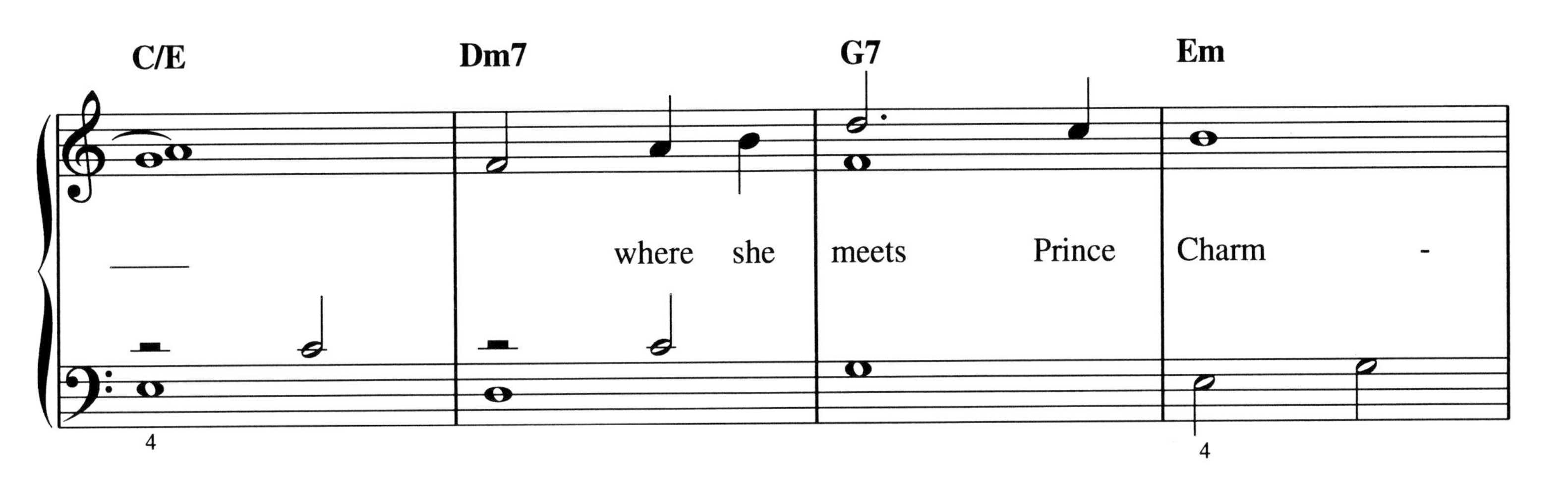
C/E
Dm7
G7
Em
where she
meets
Prince
Charm -
4
4

A9
C/D
1
2
ing,
but she
won't
dis -
cov - er

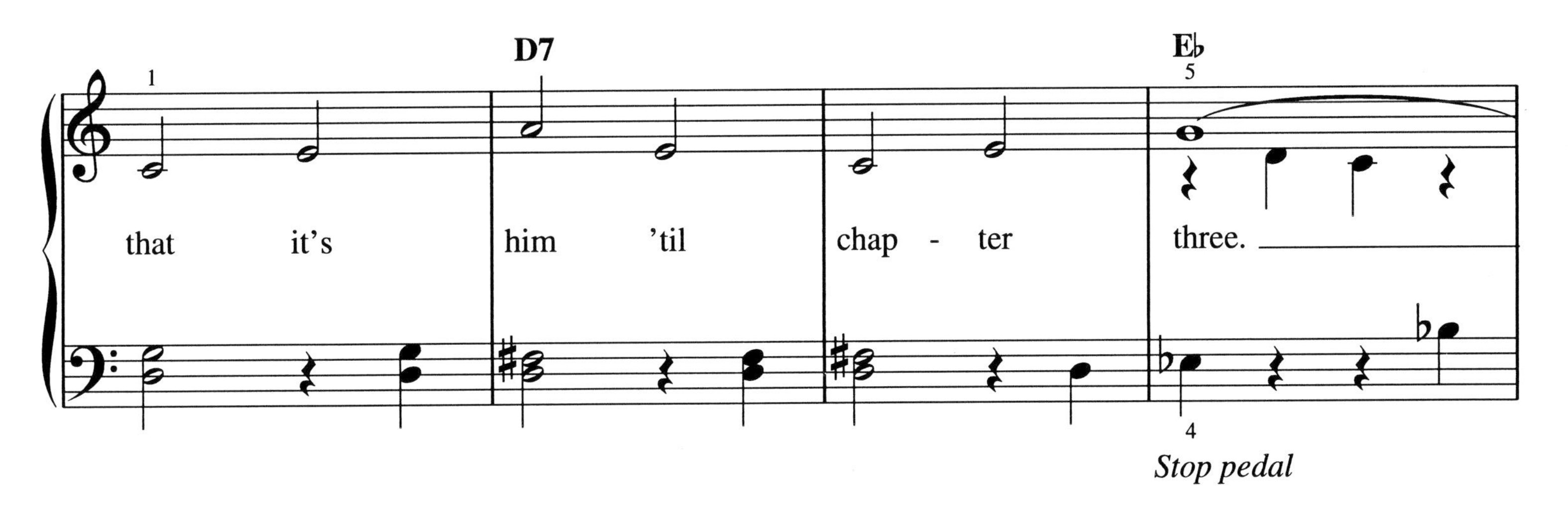
D7
E♭
1
5
that
it's
him
'til
chap - ter
three.
4
Stop pedal

Dm7
G7
C
2
Woman: Now, it's no
Townsfolk: Look there she

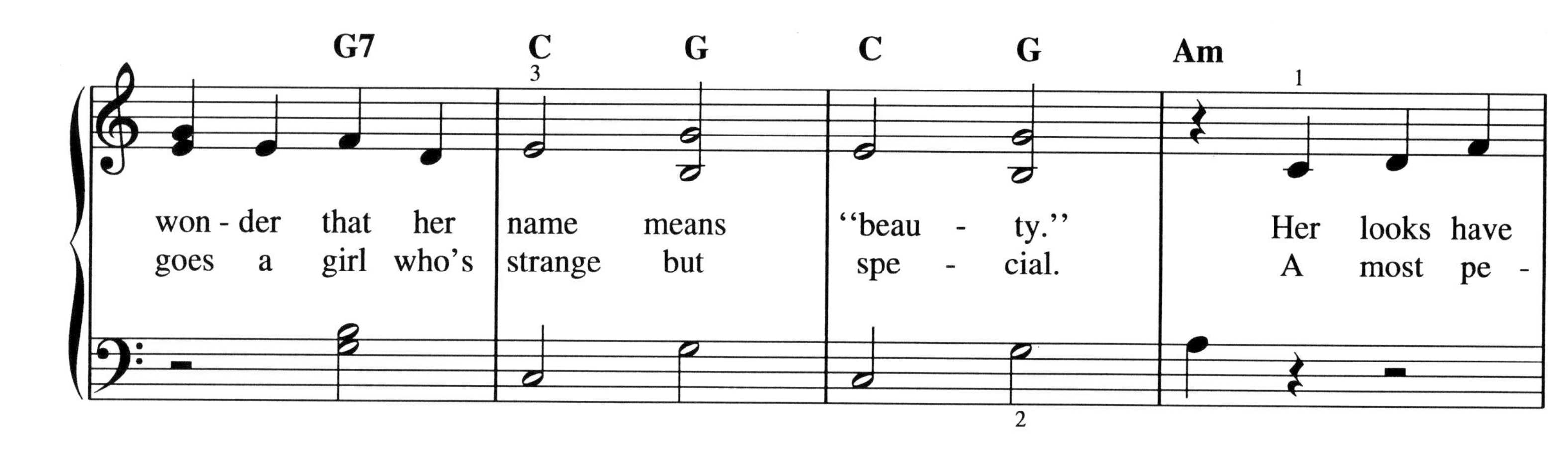
G7 C G C G Am
won - der that her name means "beau - ty." Her looks have
goes a girl who's strange but spe - cial. A most pe -

C Eb F
got no par - al - lel. Shopkeeper: But be - hind that fair fa -
cu - liar mad - 'moi - selle. It's a pit - y and a

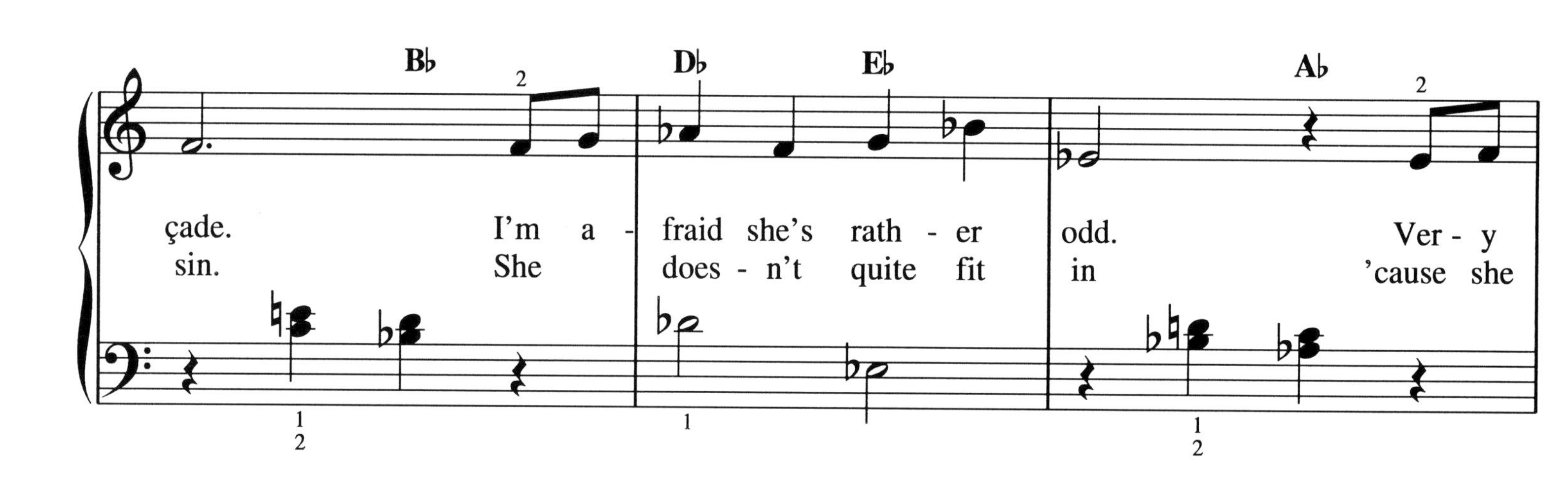
Bb Db Eb Ab
çade. I'm a - fraid she's rath - er odd. Ver - y
sin. She does - n't quite fit in 'cause she

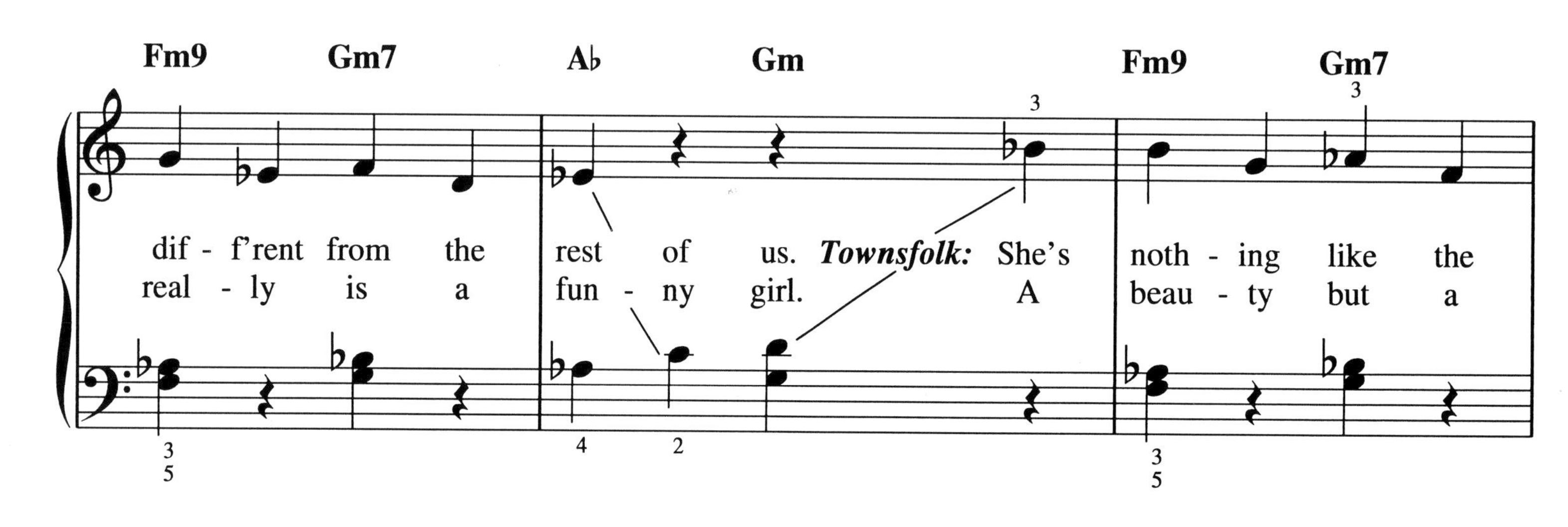
Fm9 Gm7 Ab Gm Fm9 Gm7
dif - f'rent from the rest of us. Townsfolk: She's noth - ing like the
real - ly is a fun - ny girl. A beau - ty but a

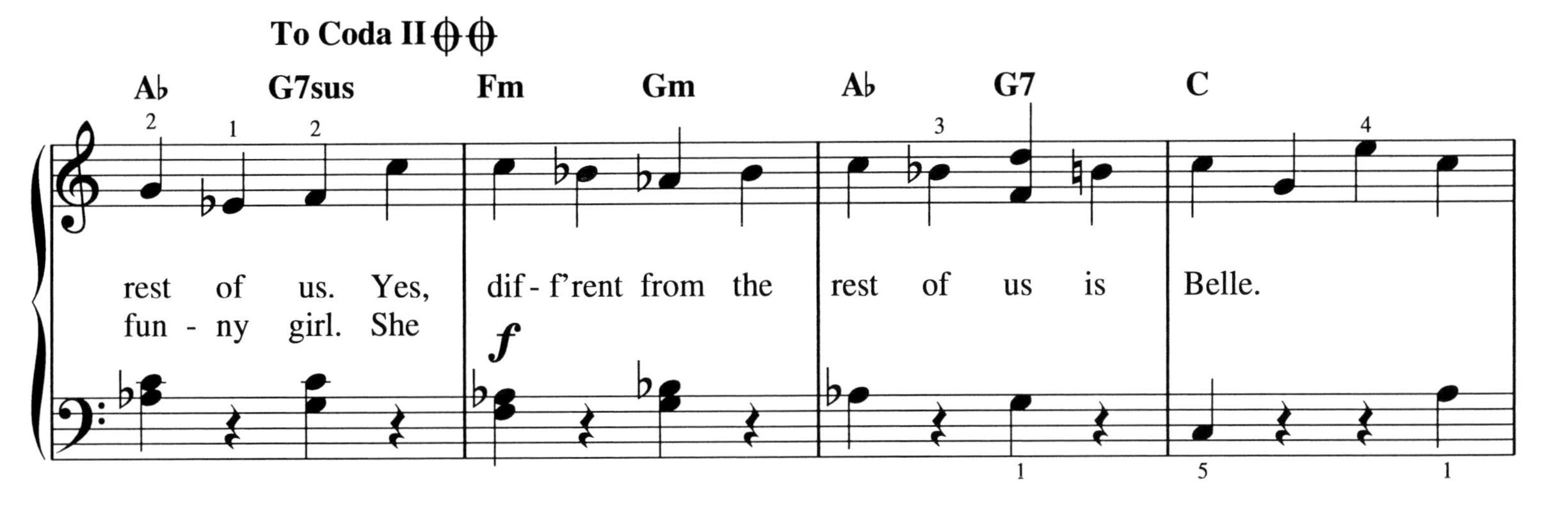
To Coda II
A♭
G7sus
Fm
Gm
A♭
G7
C
rest of us. Yes,
fun - ny girl. She
dif - f'rent from the
rest of us is
Belle.
f

Gsus
G7
C

Gsus
G7
Pompously
Gadd9
3
f
3

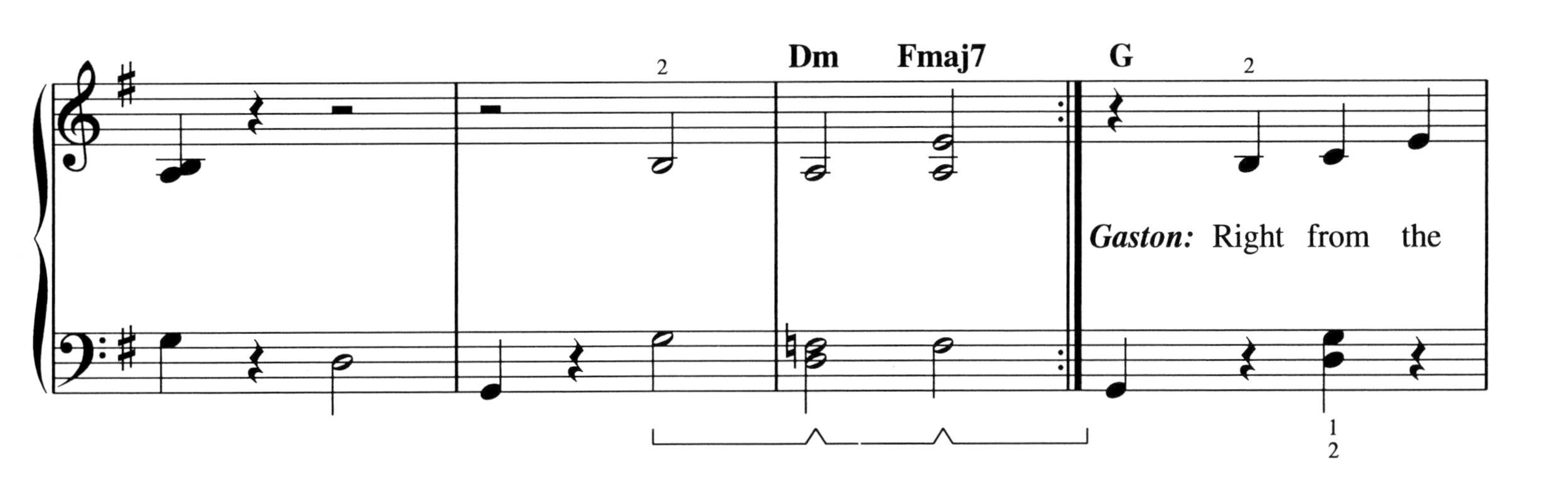
Dm
Fmaj7
G
Gaston: Right from the

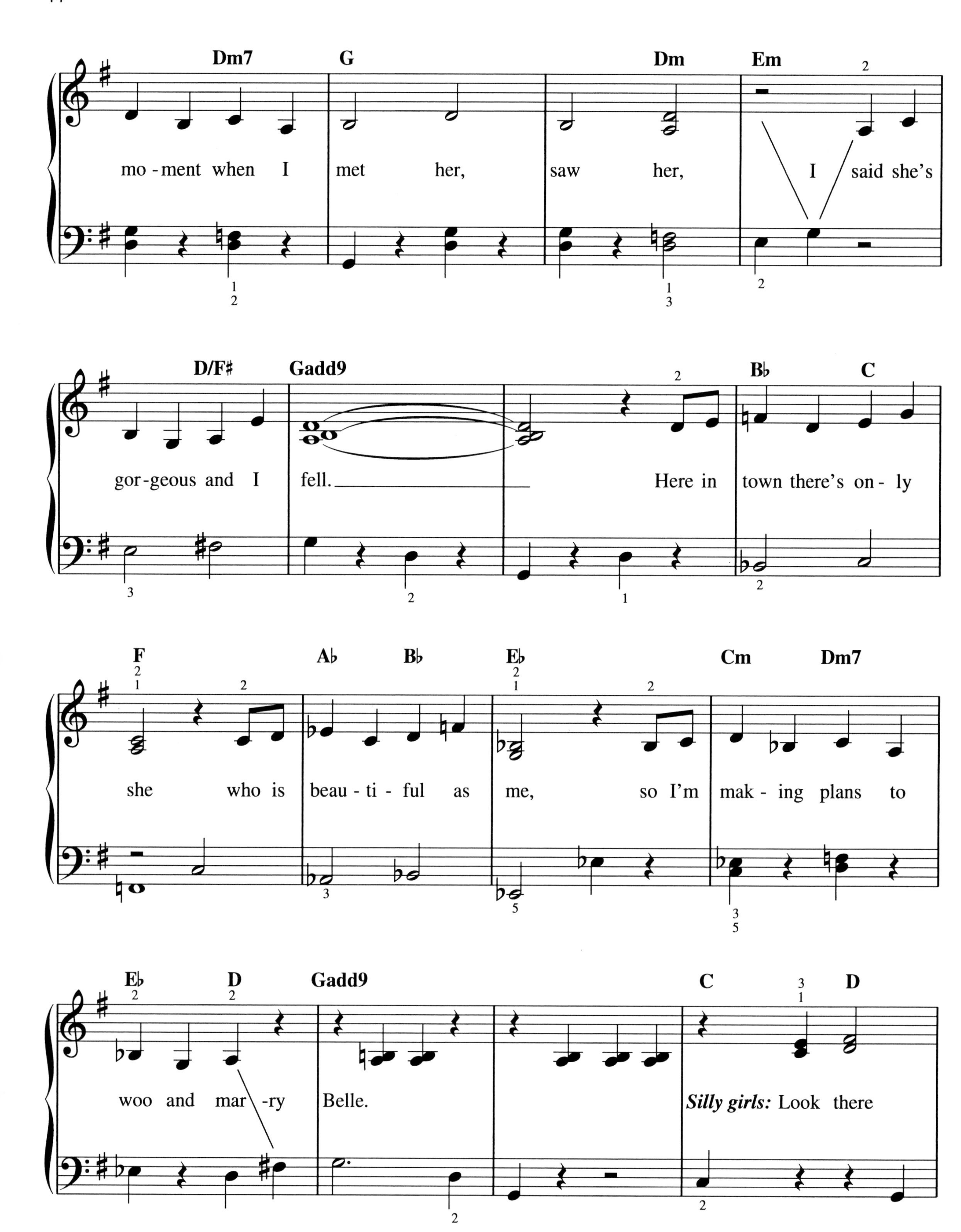
Dm7 G Dm Em
mo - ment when I met her, saw her, I said she's
D/F# Gadd9 Bb C
gor - geous and I fell. Here in town there's on - ly
F Ab Bb Eb Cm Dm7
she who is beau - ti - ful as me, so I'm mak - ing plans to
Eb D Gadd9 C D
woo and mar - ry Belle.
Silly girls: Look there

C D C D7 G/B C D
he goes! Is - n't he dream - y? Mon - sieur

C D C D7 G/B E♭ F
Gas - ton! Oh, he's so cute! Be still

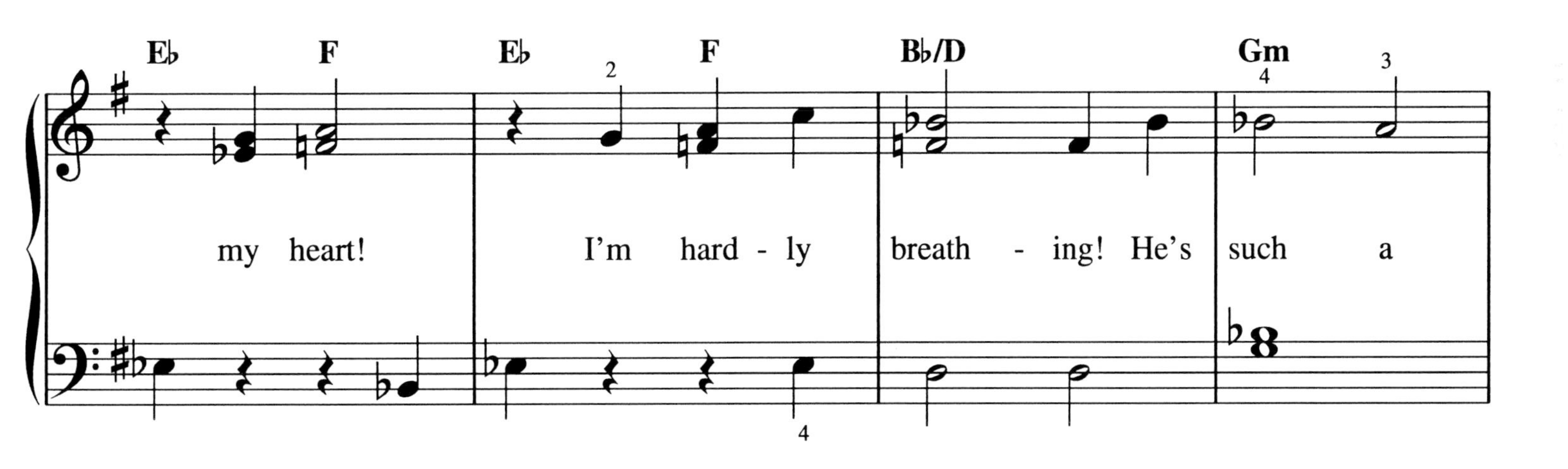
E♭ F E♭ F B♭/D Gm
my heart! I'm hard - ly breath - ing! He's such a

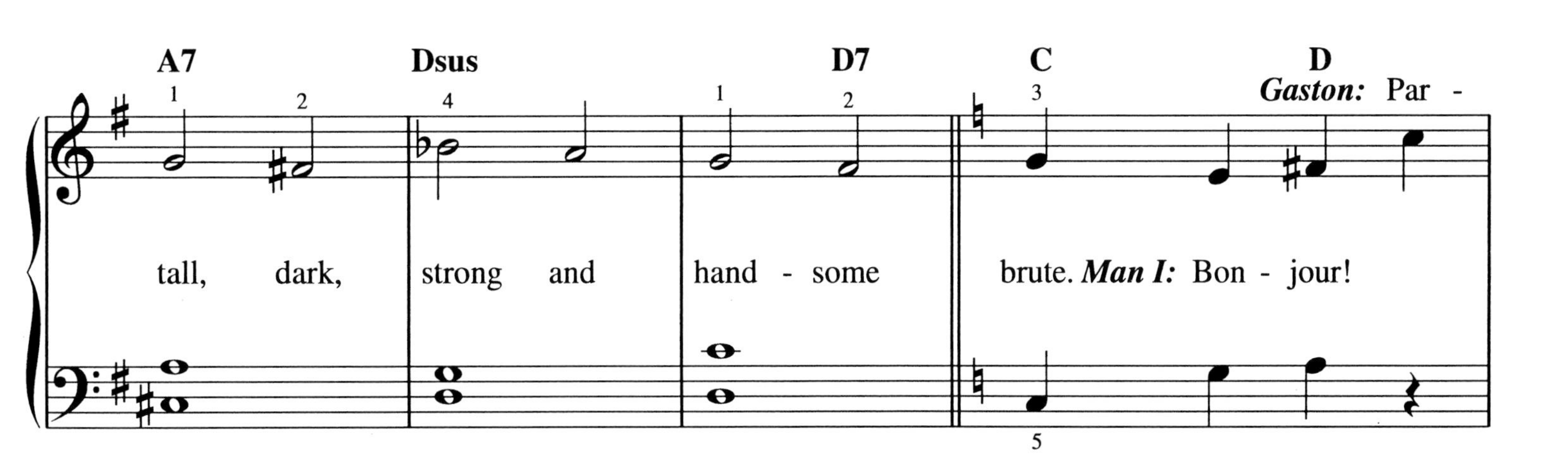
A7 Dsus D7 C D
Gaston: Par -
tall, dark, strong and hand - some brute. Man I: Bon - jour!

C D C D G/B C D
don. Man III: Mais oui! Woman I: What love - ly grapes! Woman II: Ten
Man II: Good day. Matron: You call this ba - con? Man IV: Some cheese...

C D C D G/B E♭ F
yards. Gaston: 'Scuse me! Please let me through! Man IV: Those
...one pound. Cheese merchant: I'll get the knife. Woman I: This bread...
E♭ F E♭ F B♭/D
fish... ...they smell!
...it's stale! Baker: Ma - dame's mis - tak - en. Belle: There

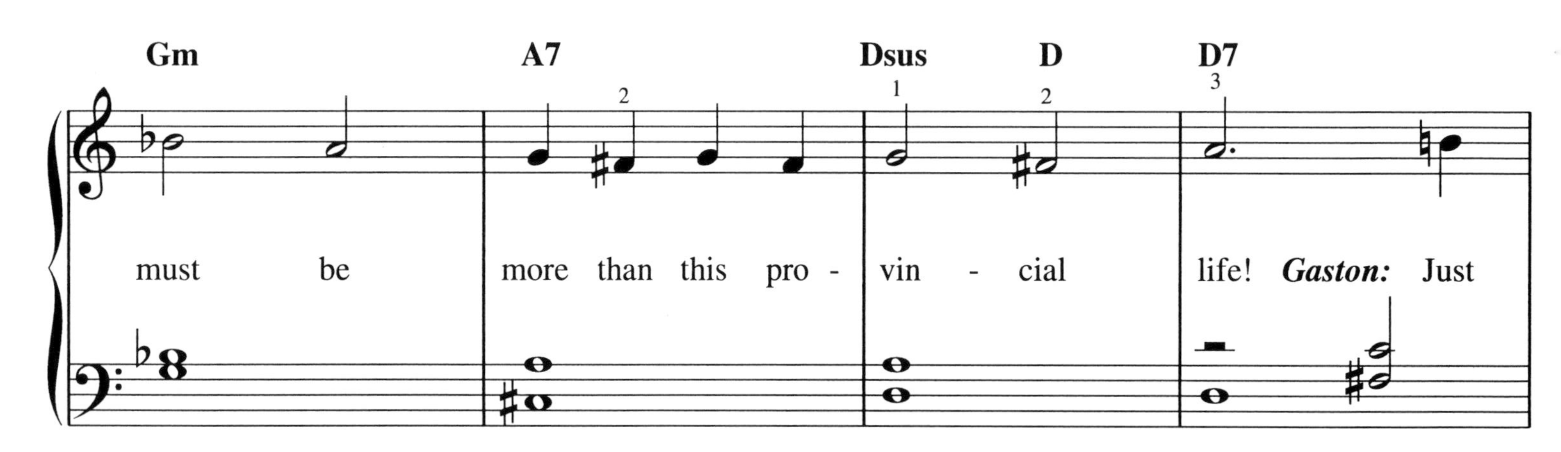
Gm A7 Dsus D D7
must be more than this pro - vin - cial life! Gaston: Just

F/G
G7
D.S.S. al Coda II
watch I'm go - ing to make Belle my wife!

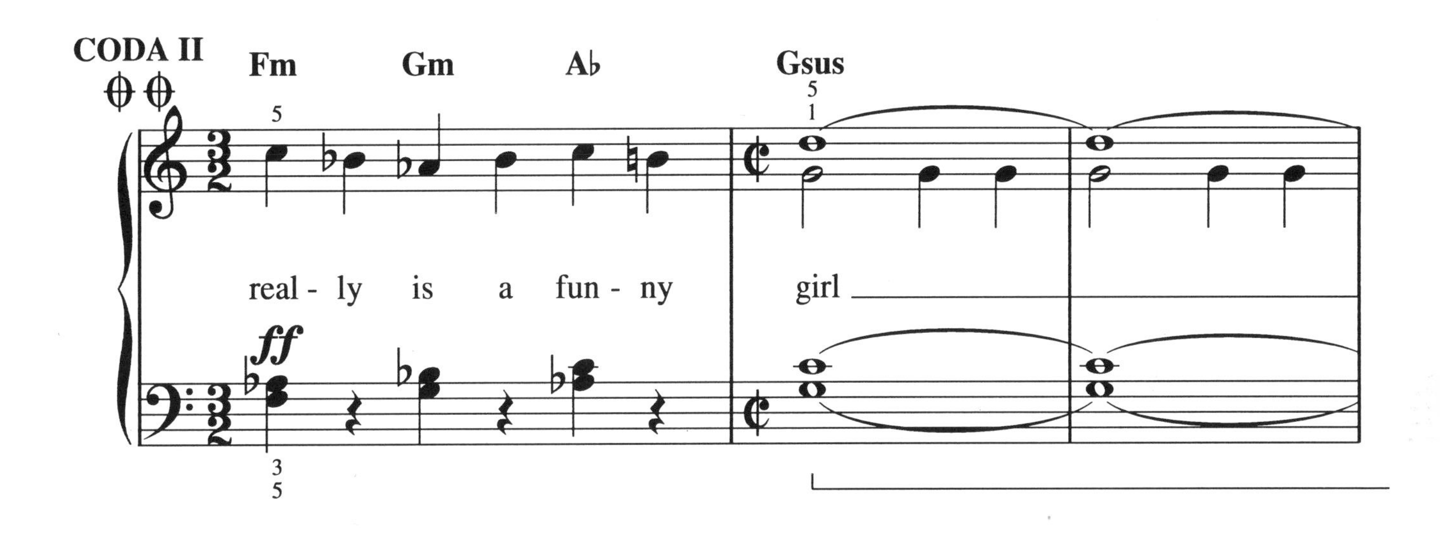
CODA II
Fm
Gm
A♭
Gsus
real - ly is a fun - ny girl
ff

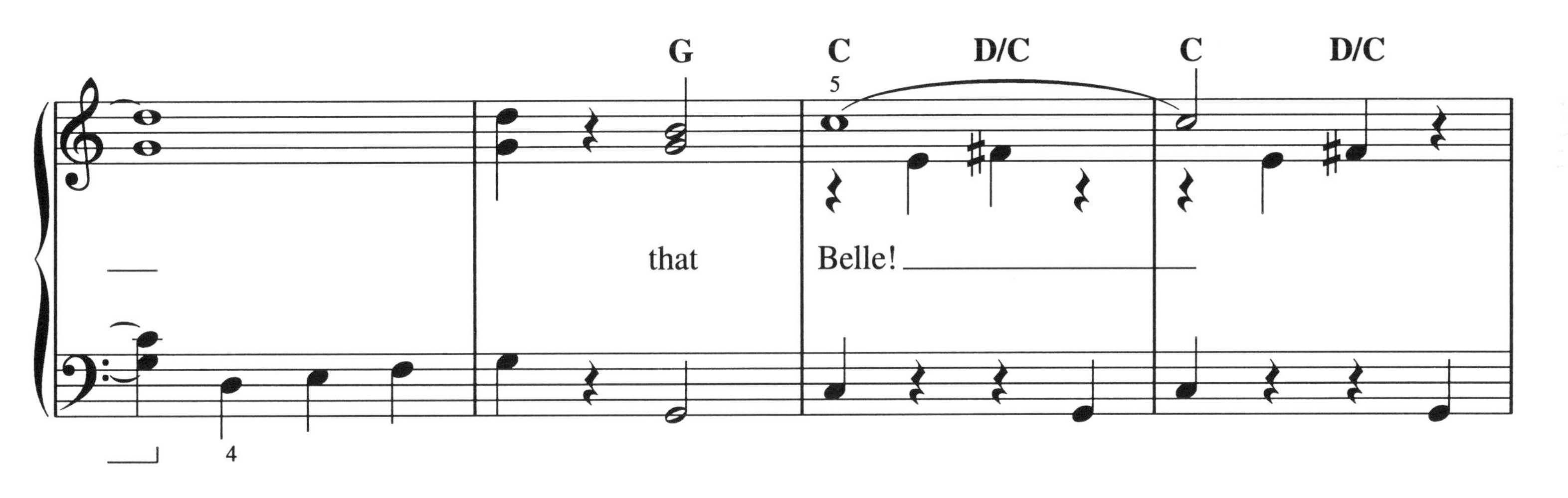
G
C
D/C
C
D/C
that Belle!

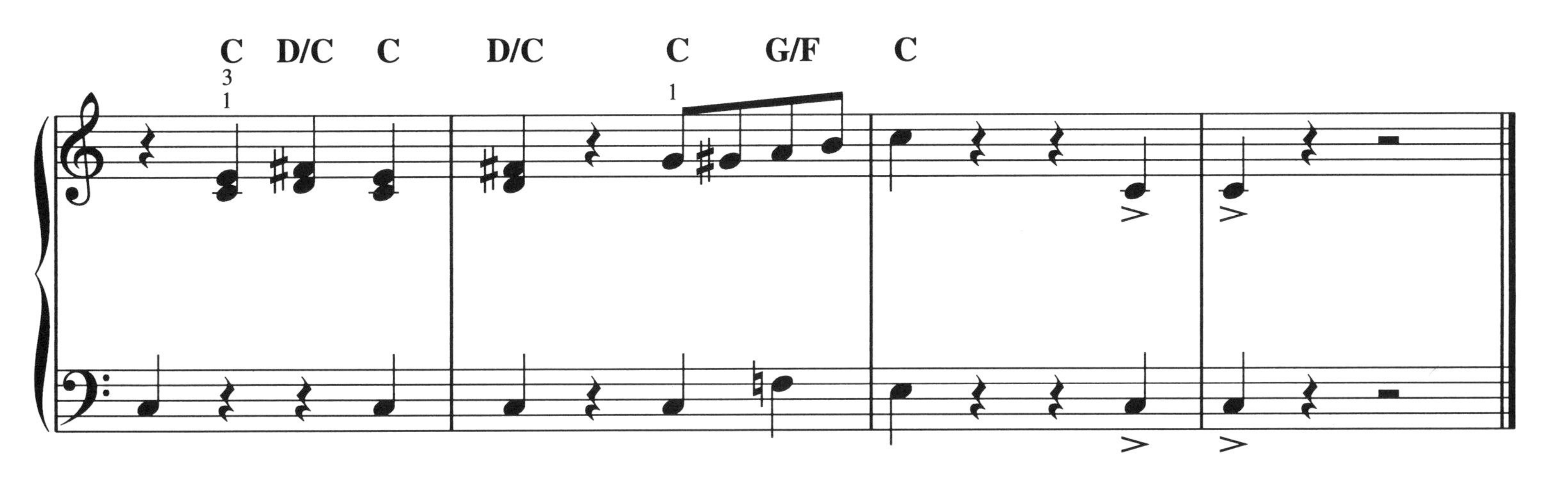
C
D/C
C
D/C
C
G/F
C

BELLE
(Reprise)

Lyrics by HOWARD ASHMAN
Music by ALAN MENKEN

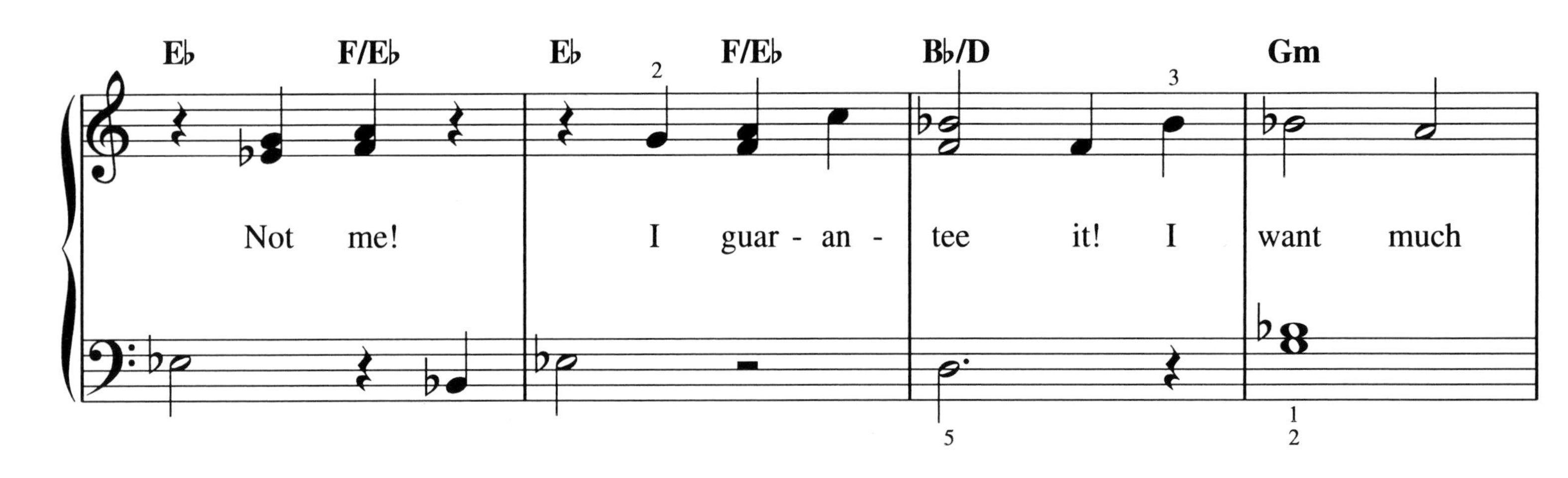
E♭
F/E♭
E♭
F/E♭
B♭/D
Gm
Not me!
I guar - an - tee it! I want much

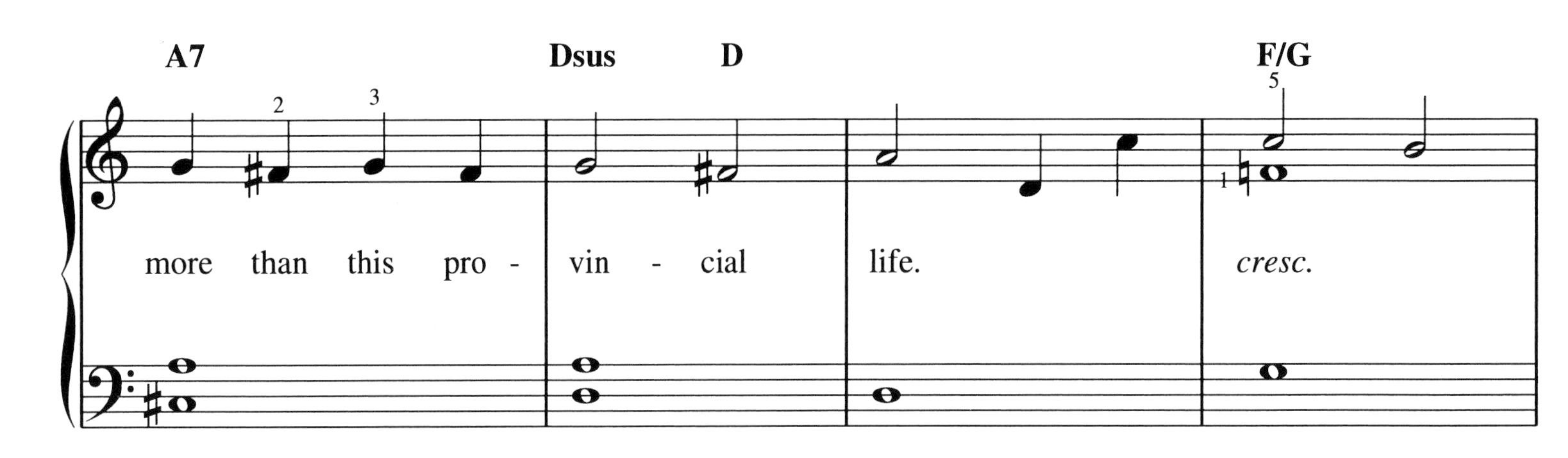
A7
Dsus
D
F/G
more than this pro - vin - cial life.
cresc.

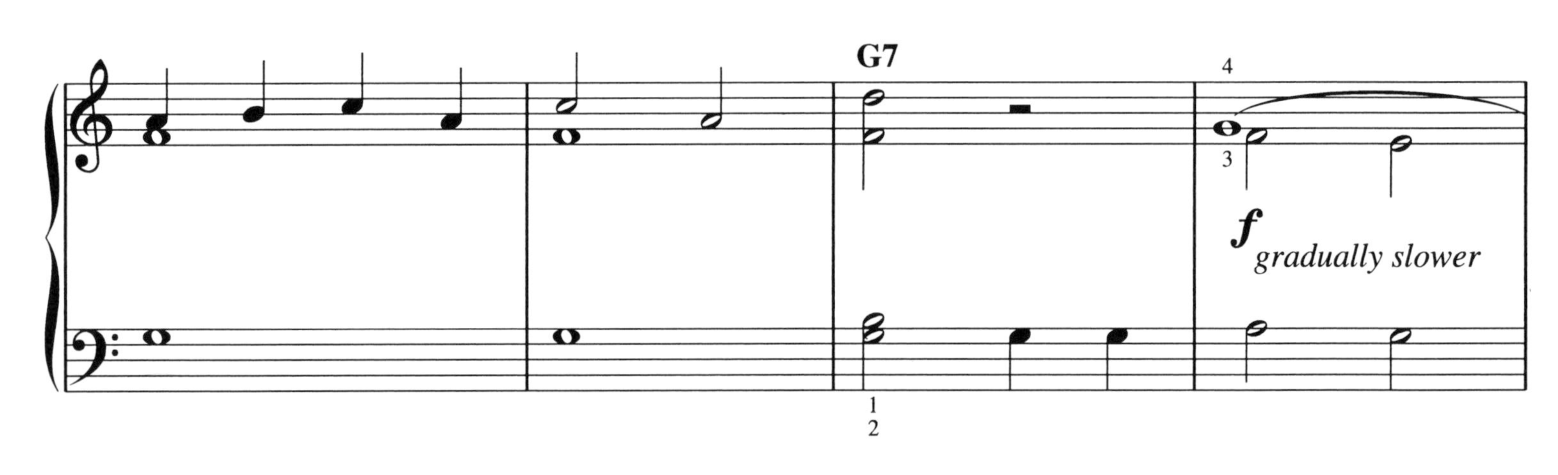
G7
f
gradually slower

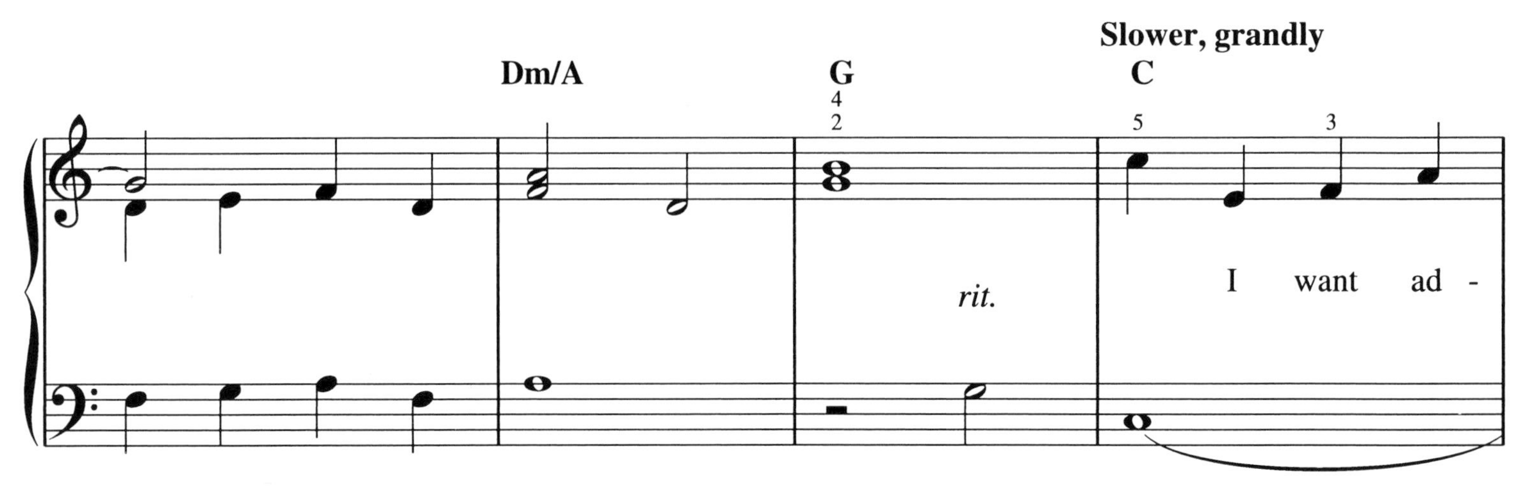
Slower, grandly
Dm/A
G
C
rit.
I want ad -

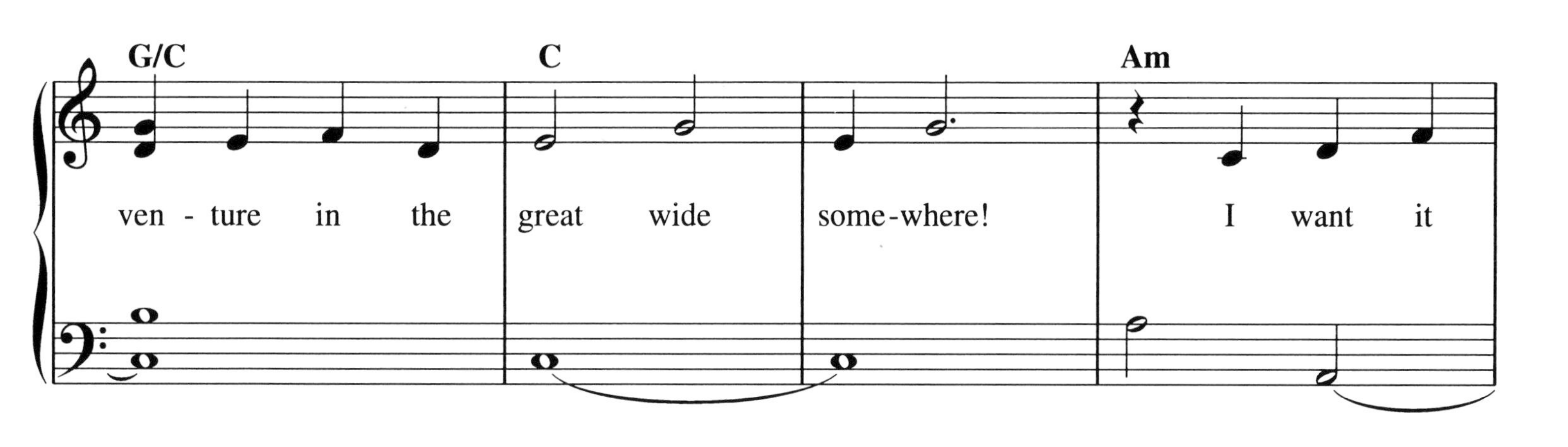
G/C
C
Am
ven - ture in the great wide some-where! I want it

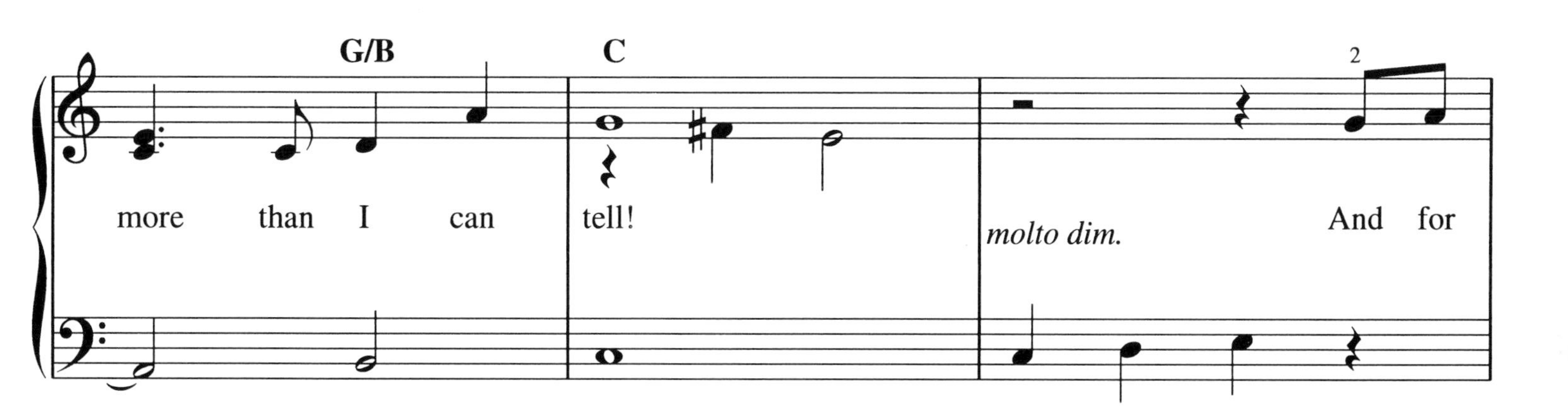
G/B
C
more than I can tell!
molto dim.
And for

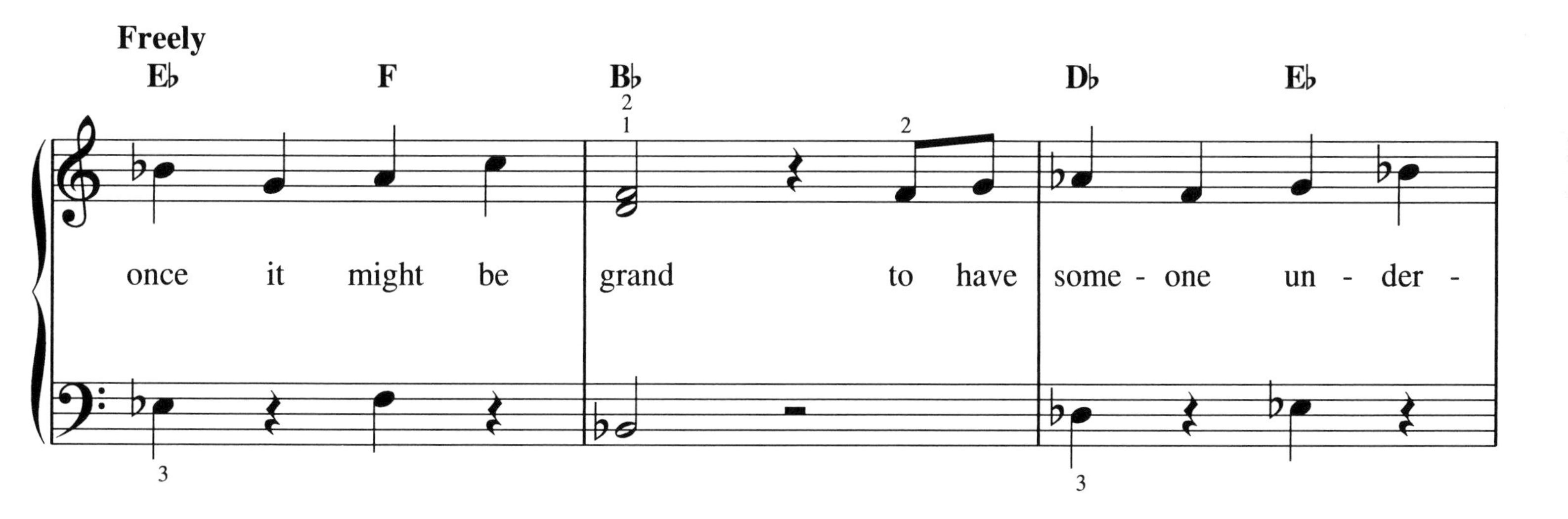
Freely
E♭
F
B♭
D♭
E♭
once it might be grand to have some - one un - der -

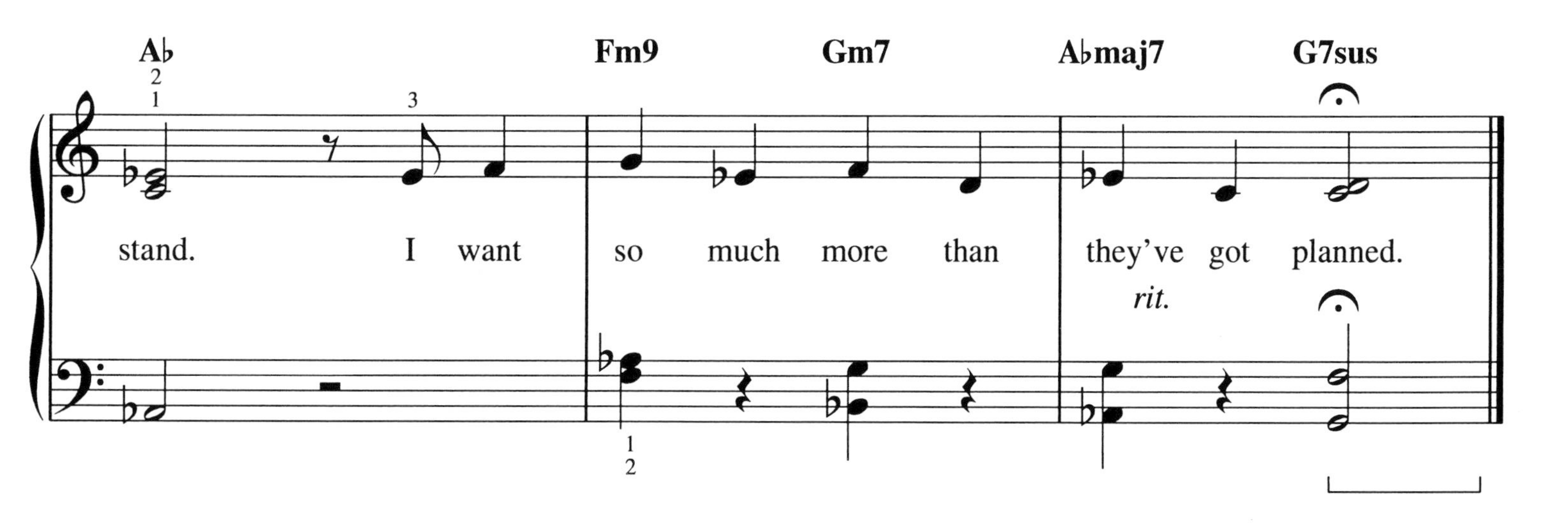
A♭
Fm9
Gm7
A♭maj7
G7sus
stand. I want so much more than they've got planned.
rit.

GASTON

Lyrics by HOWARD ASHMAN
Music by ALAN MENKEN

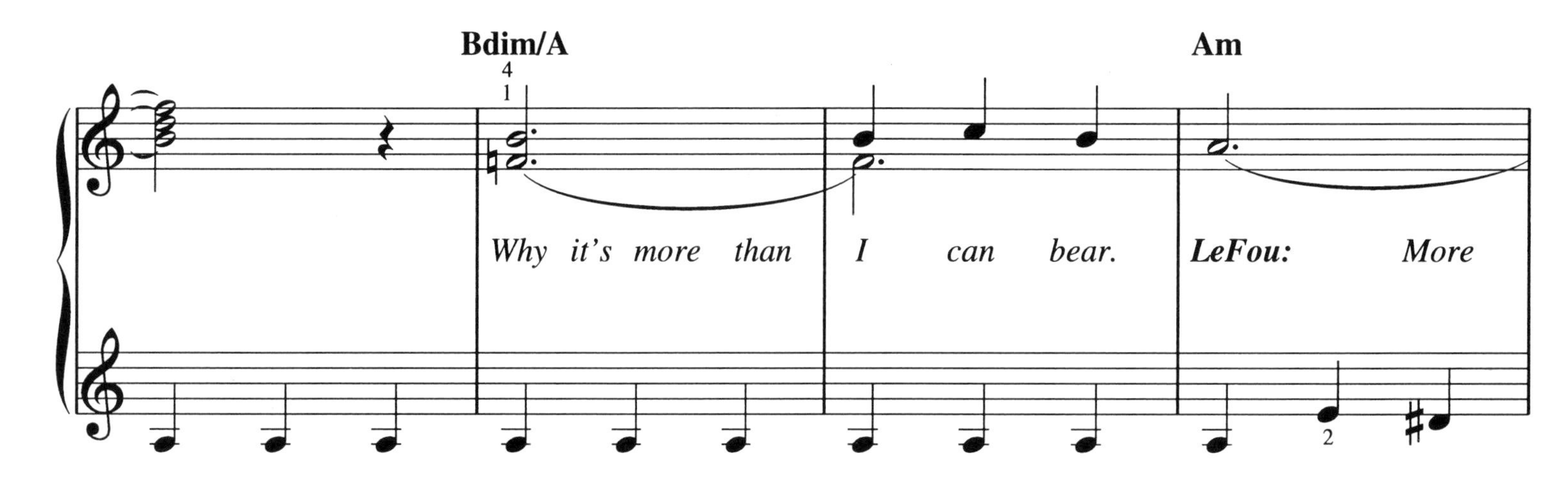
Bdim/A
Am
Why it's more than I can bear.
LeFou: More

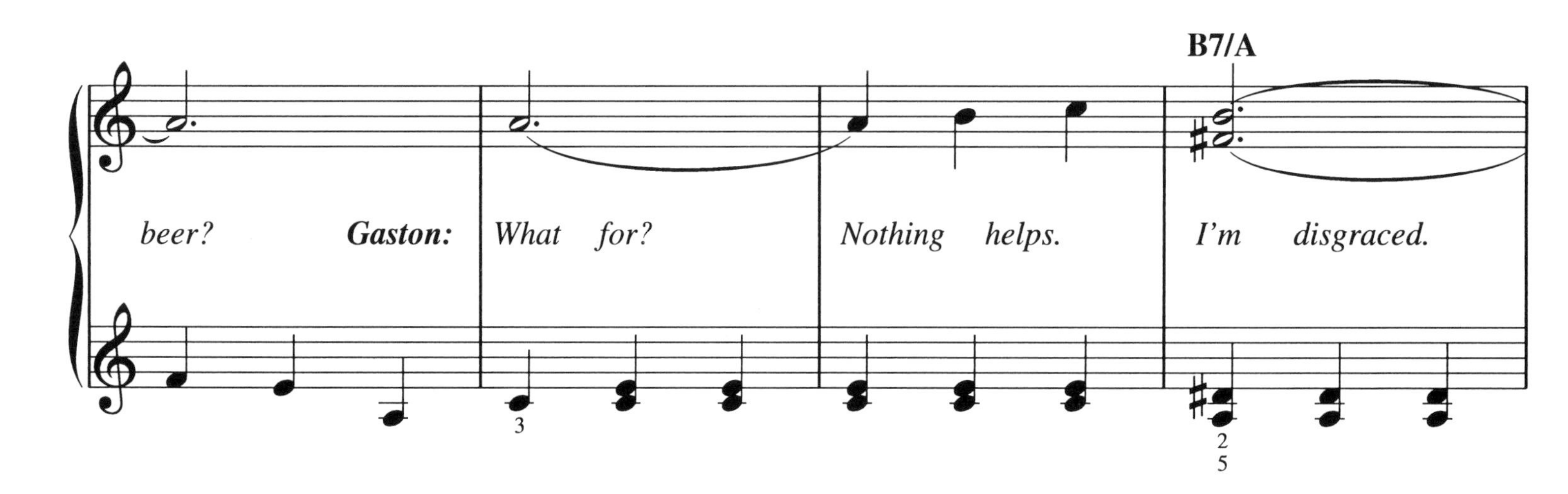
B7/A
beer? Gaston: What for? Nothing helps. I'm disgraced.

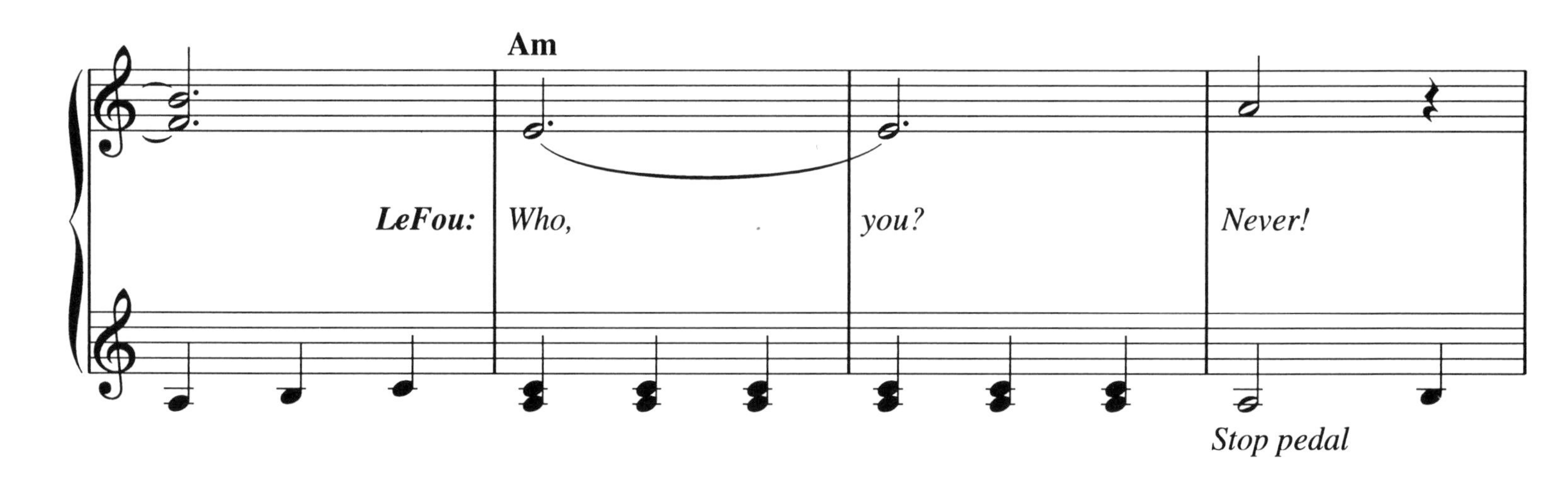
Am
LeFou: Who, you? Never!
Stop pedal

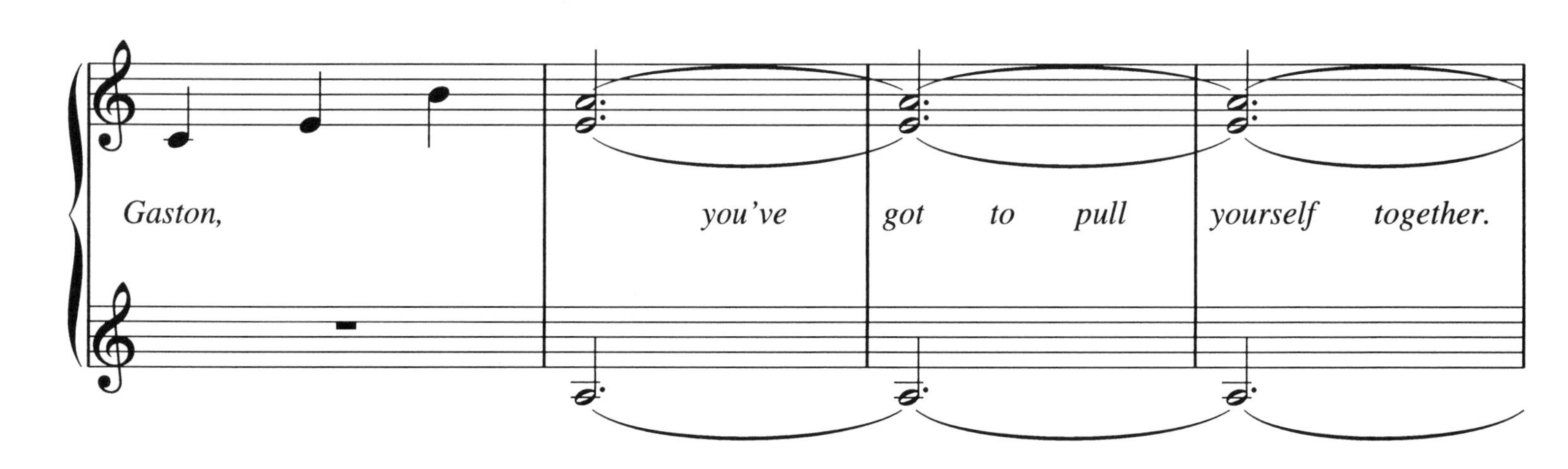
Gaston, you've got to pull yourself together.

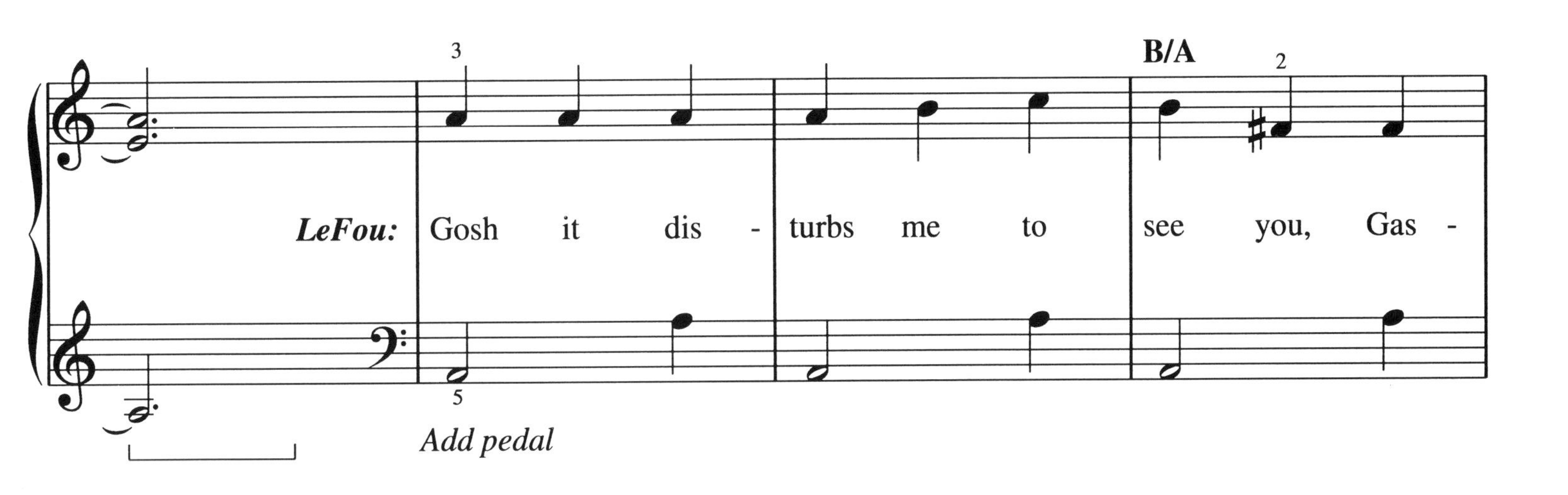
B/A
LeFou:
Gosh it dis - turbs me to see you, Gas -
Add pedal

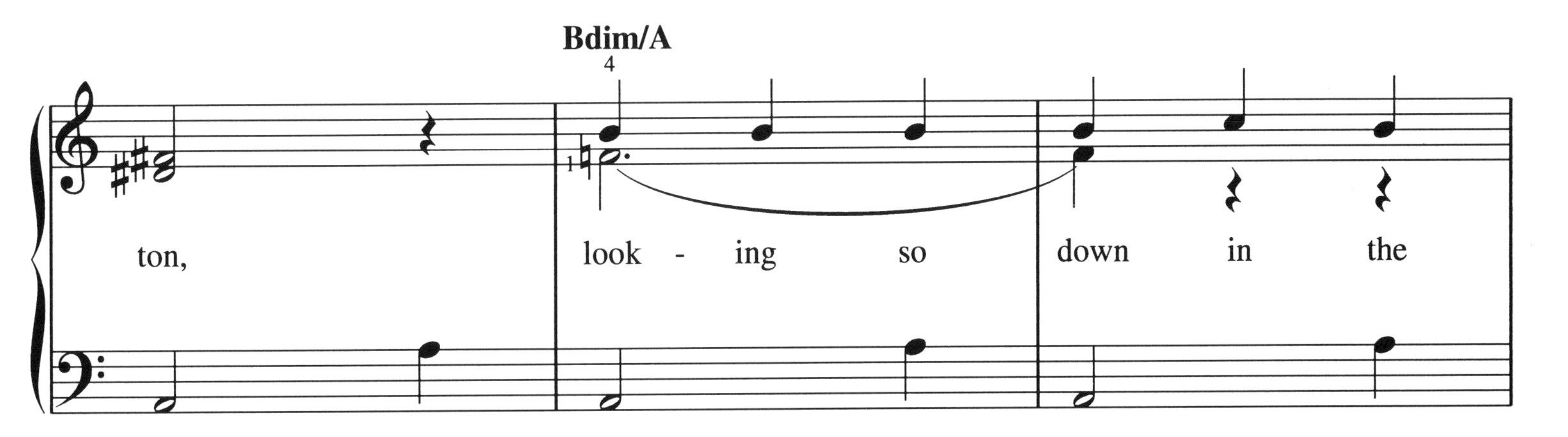
Bdim/A
ton, look - ing so down in the

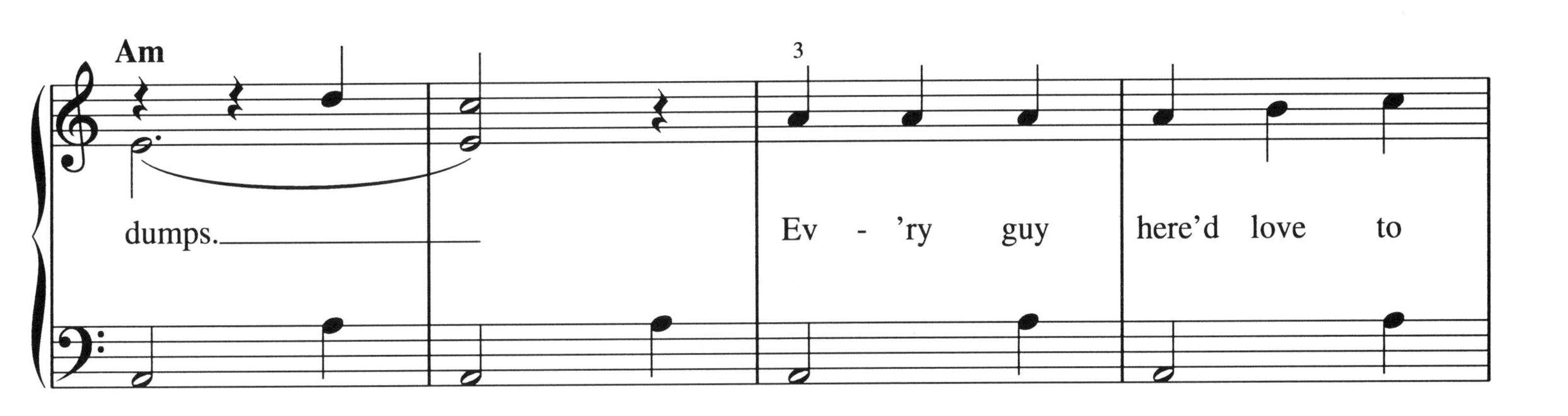
Am
dumps. Ev - 'ry guy here'd love to

B/A
Bdim/A
be you, Gas - ton, e - ven when

Am
tak - ing your lumps.
There's

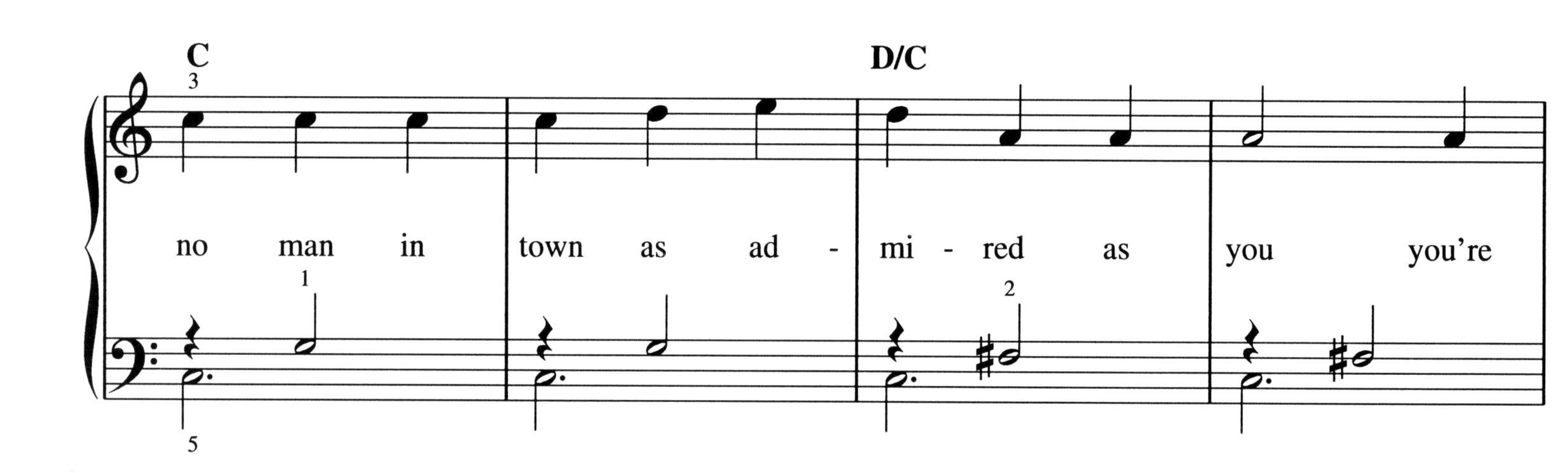
C
D/C
no man in town as ad - mi - red as you you're

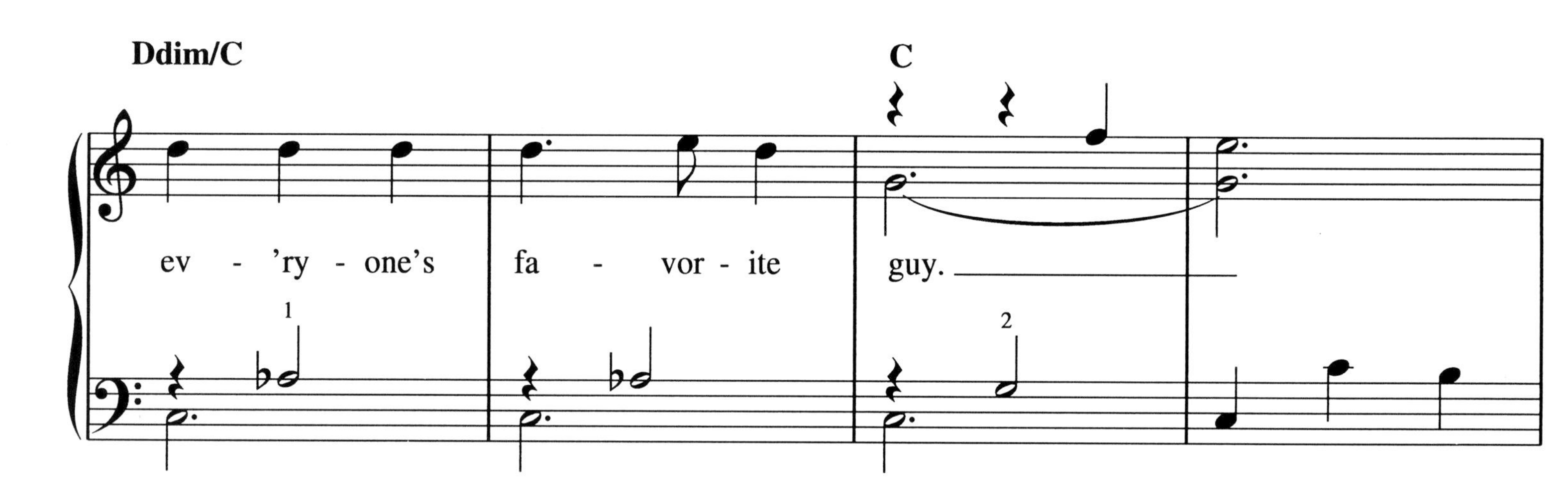
Ddim/C
C
ev - 'ry - one's fa - vor - ite guy.

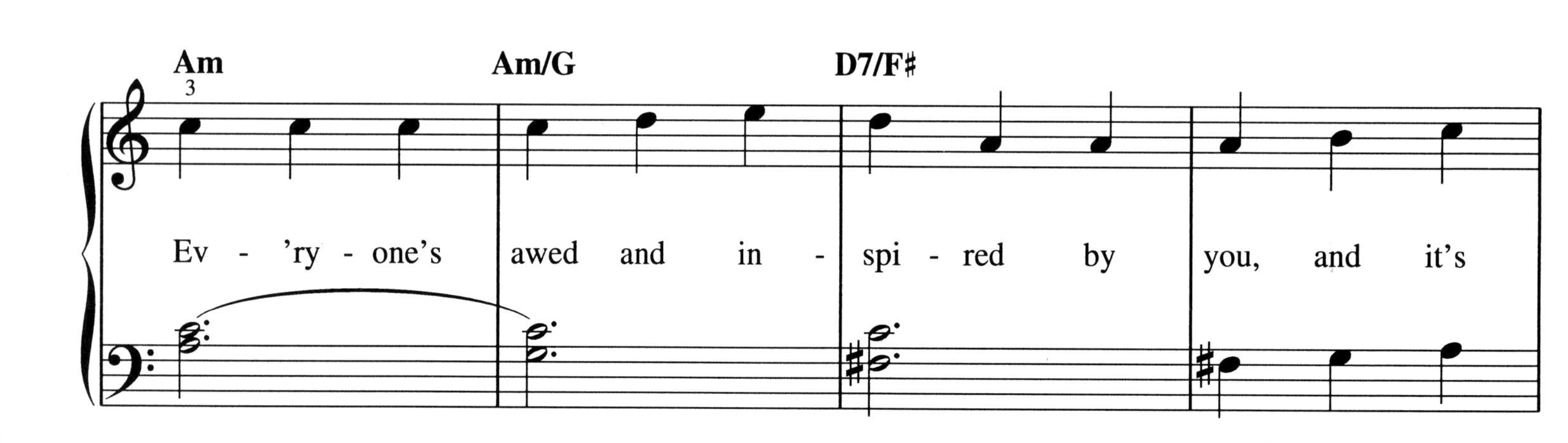
Am
Am/G
D7/F#
Ev - 'ry - one's awed and in - spi - red by you, and it's

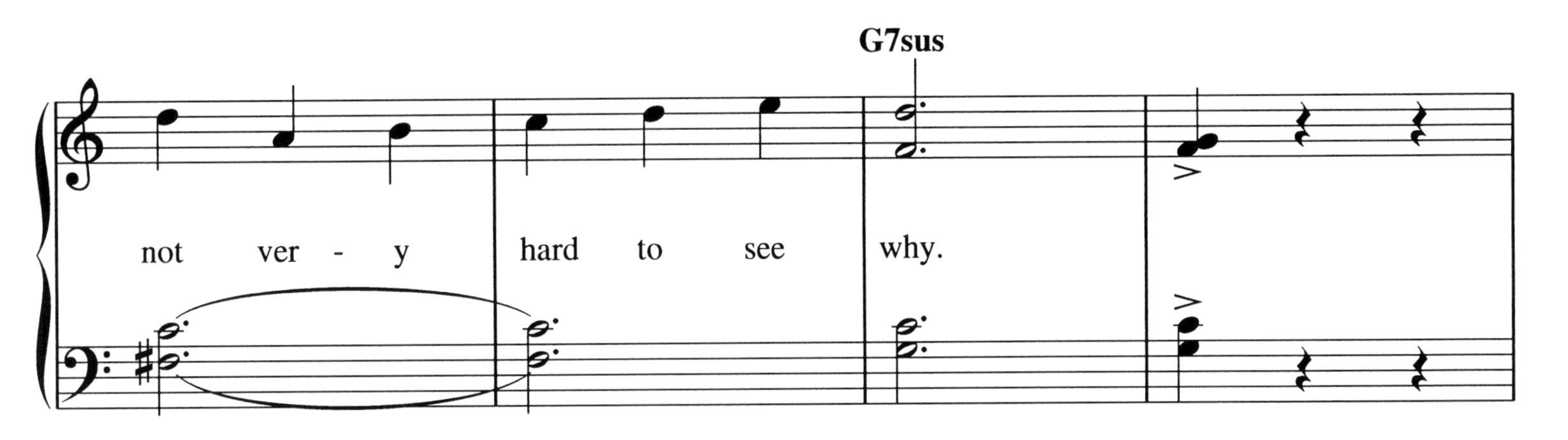
G7sus
not ver - y hard to see why.

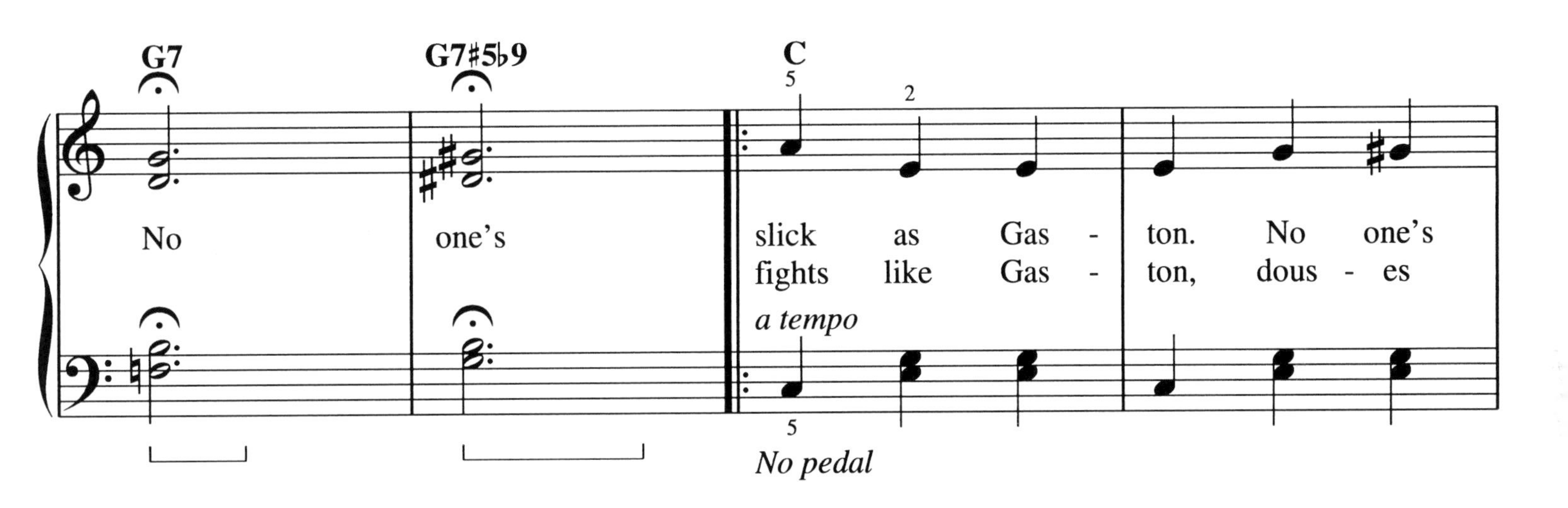
G7
G7♯5♭9
C
No one's slick as Gas - ton. No one's
fights like Gas - ton, dous - es
a tempo
No pedal

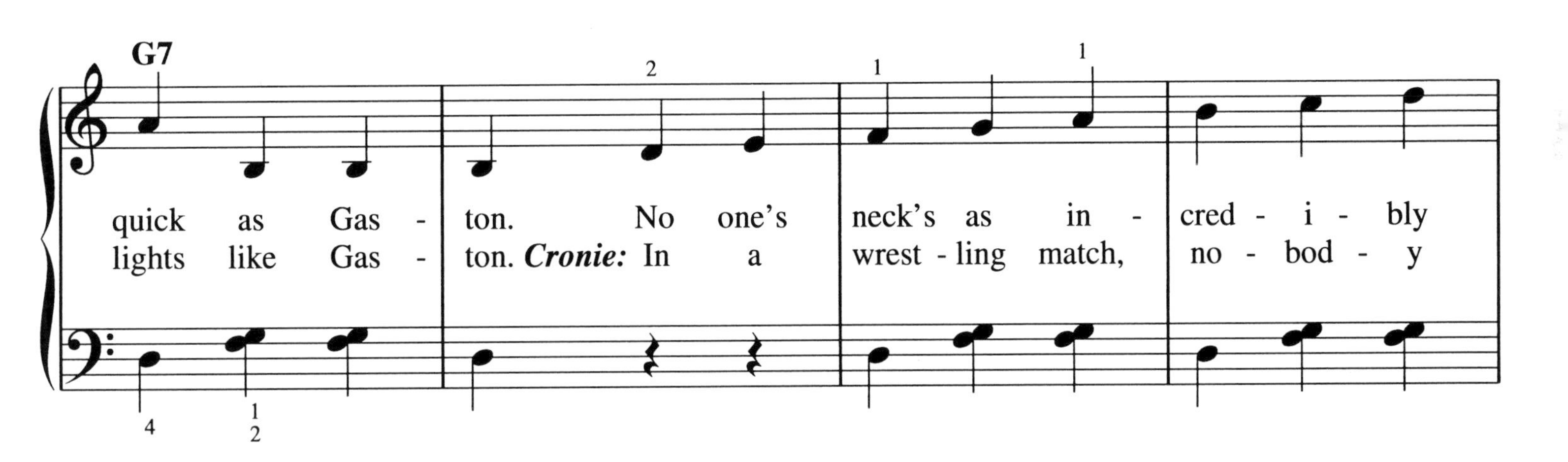
G7
quick as Gas - ton. No one's neck's as in - cred - i - bly
lights like Gas - ton. Cronie: In a wrest - ling match, no - bod - y

C
Am
thick as Gas - ton! For there's no man in town half as
bites like Gas - ton! Girls: For there's no one as bur - ly and

Dm7
G7
man - ly.
brawn - y.
Gaston: As you
Per - fect! A
see, I've got
pure par - a -
bi - ceps to

C6
Am
gon!
spare.
You can
LeFou: Not a
ask an - y
bit of him's
Tom, Dick, or
scrag - gly or

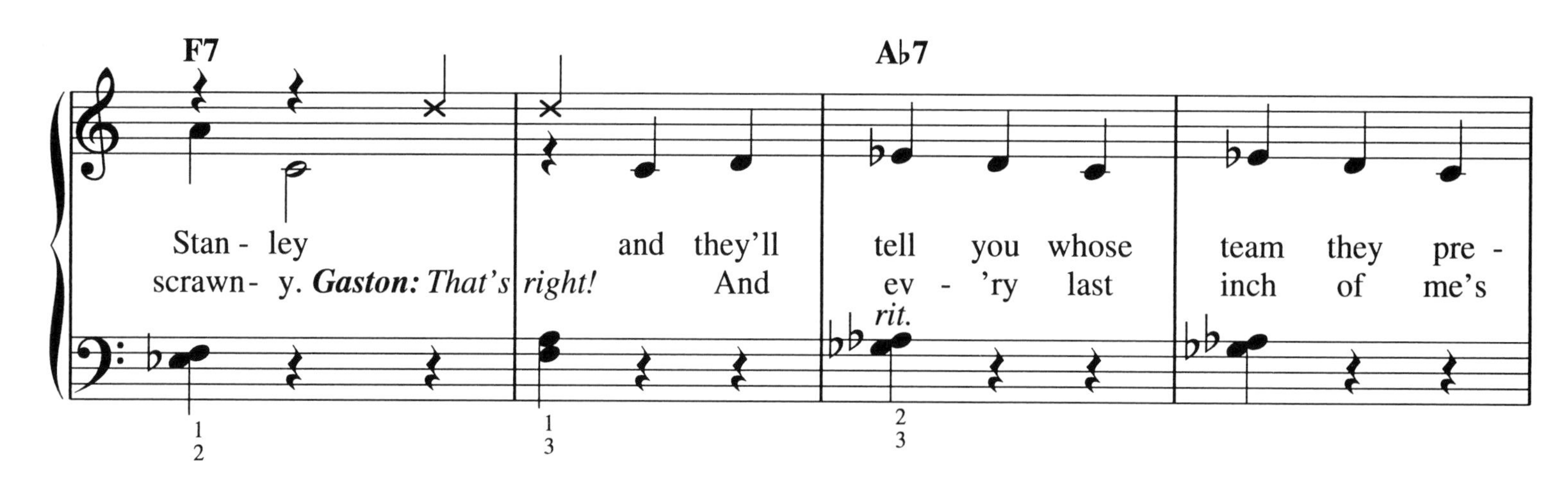
F7
A♭7
Stan - ley
scrawn- y. Gaston: That's right!
and they'll
And
tell you whose
ev - 'ry last
rit.
team they pre -
inch of me's

G7
G7♯5♭9
fer to be
cov - ered with
on! Chorus:
hair! Cronies:
Chorus:
No -
No -
No -
one's
one
one

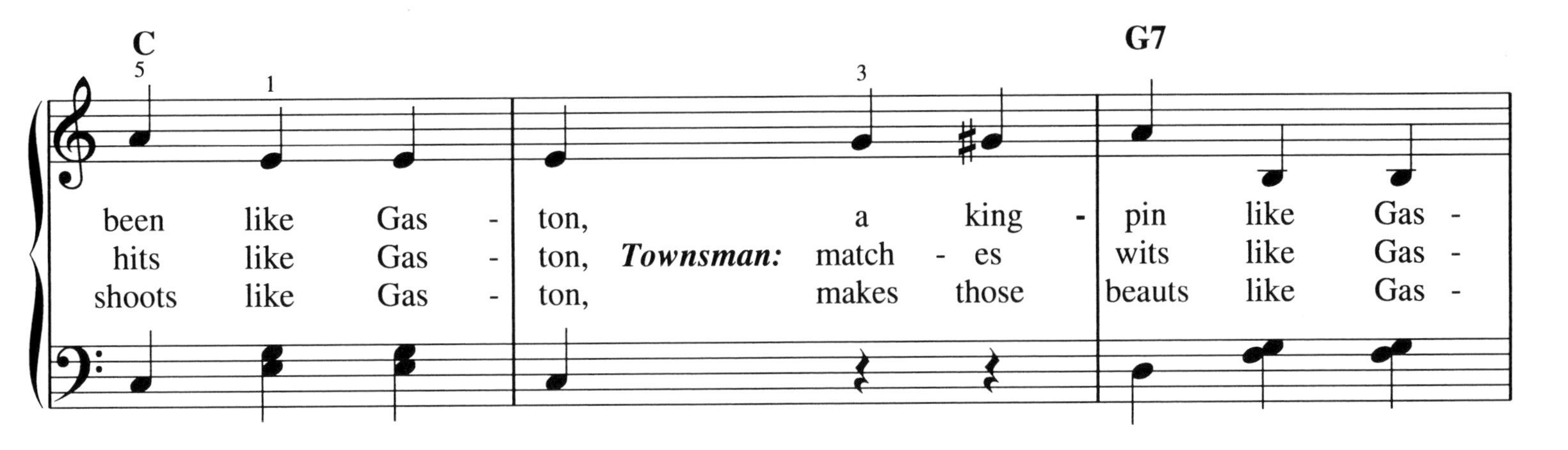
C
G7
been like Gas - ton, a king - pin like Gas -
hits like Gas - ton, Townsman: match - es wits like Gas -
shoots like Gas - ton, makes those beauts like Gas -

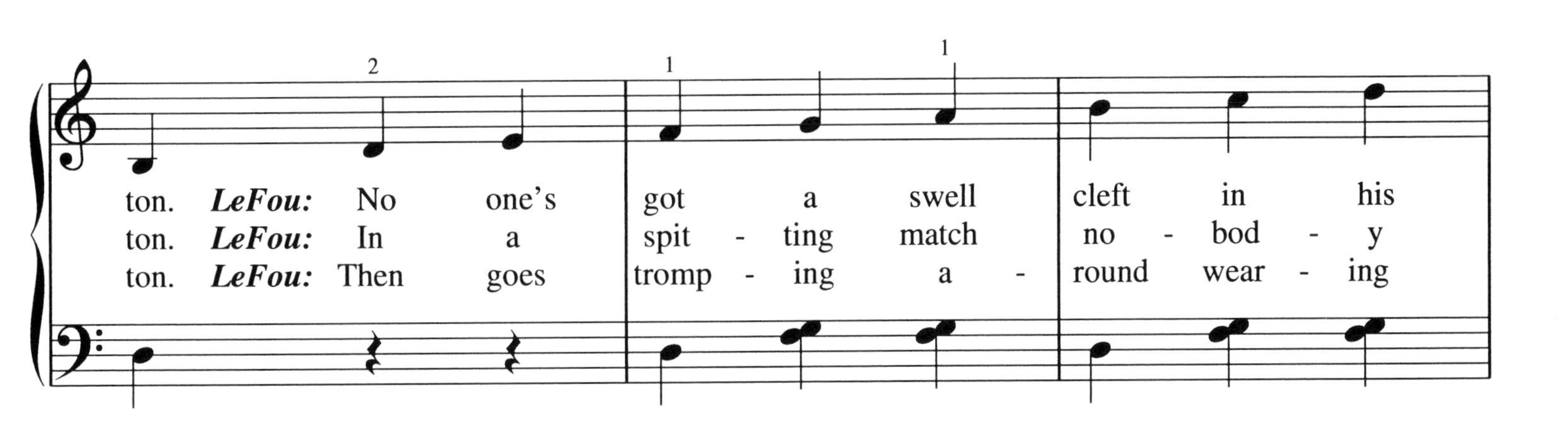
ton. LeFou: No one's got a swell cleft in his
ton. LeFou: In a spit - ting match no - bod - y
ton. LeFou: Then goes tromp - ing a - round wear - ing

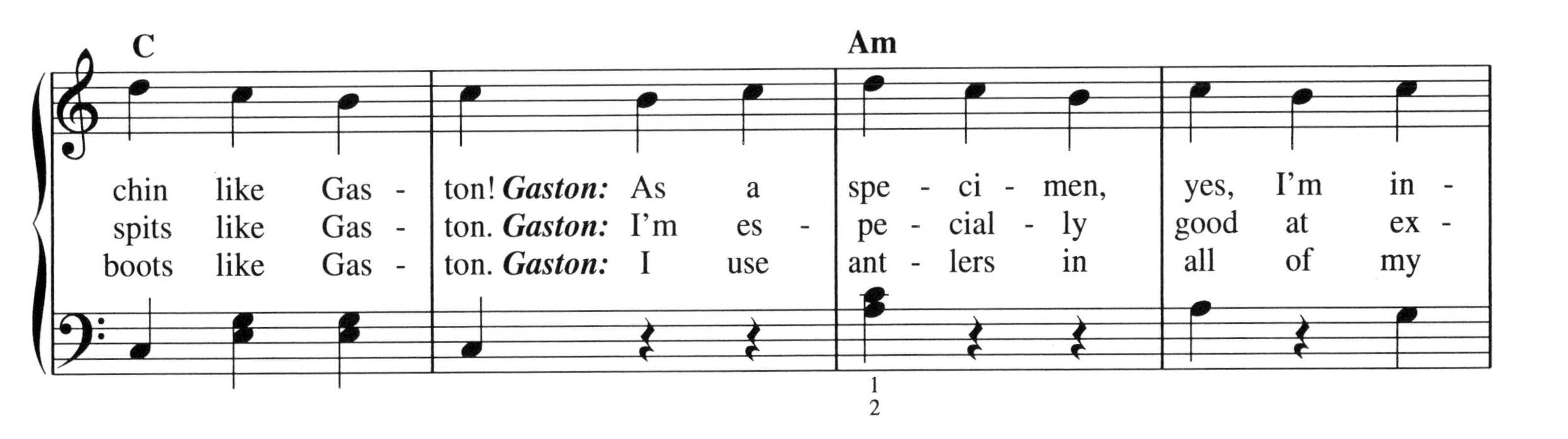
C
Am
chin like Gas - ton! Gaston: As a spe - ci - men, yes, I'm in -
spits like Gas - ton. Gaston: I'm es - pe - cial - ly good at ex -
boots like Gas - ton. Gaston: I use ant - lers in all of my

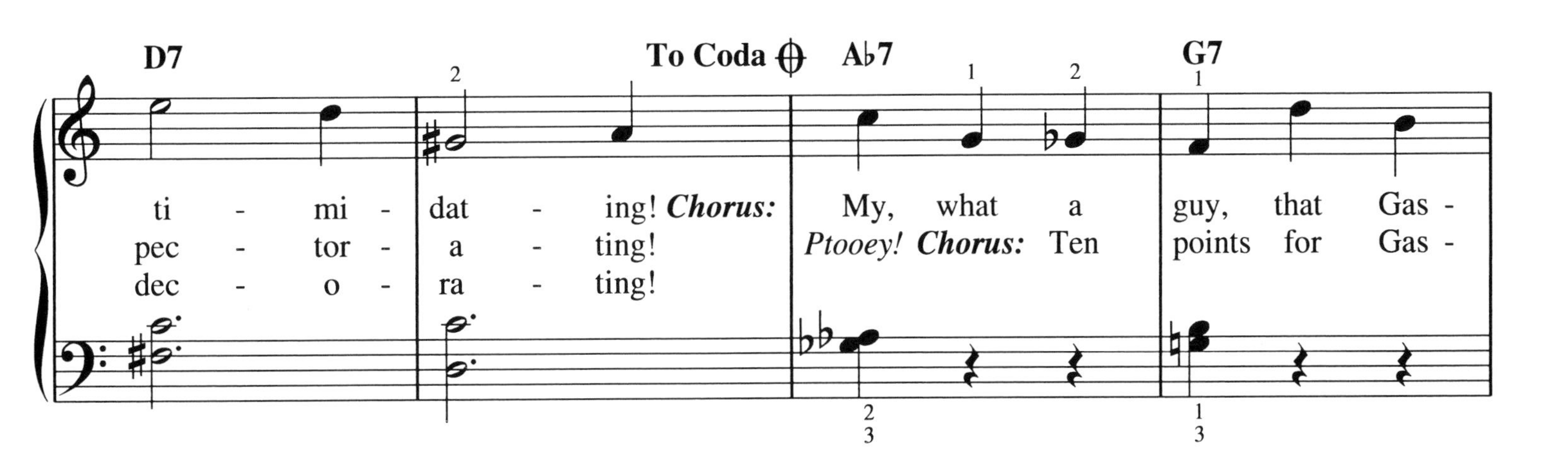
D7
To Coda
A♭7
G7
ti - mi - dat - ing! Chorus: My, what a guy, that Gas -
pec - tor - a - ting! Ptooey! Chorus: Ten points for Gas -
dec - o - ra - ting!

1
C
G
ton! Give five "hur - rahs!" Give

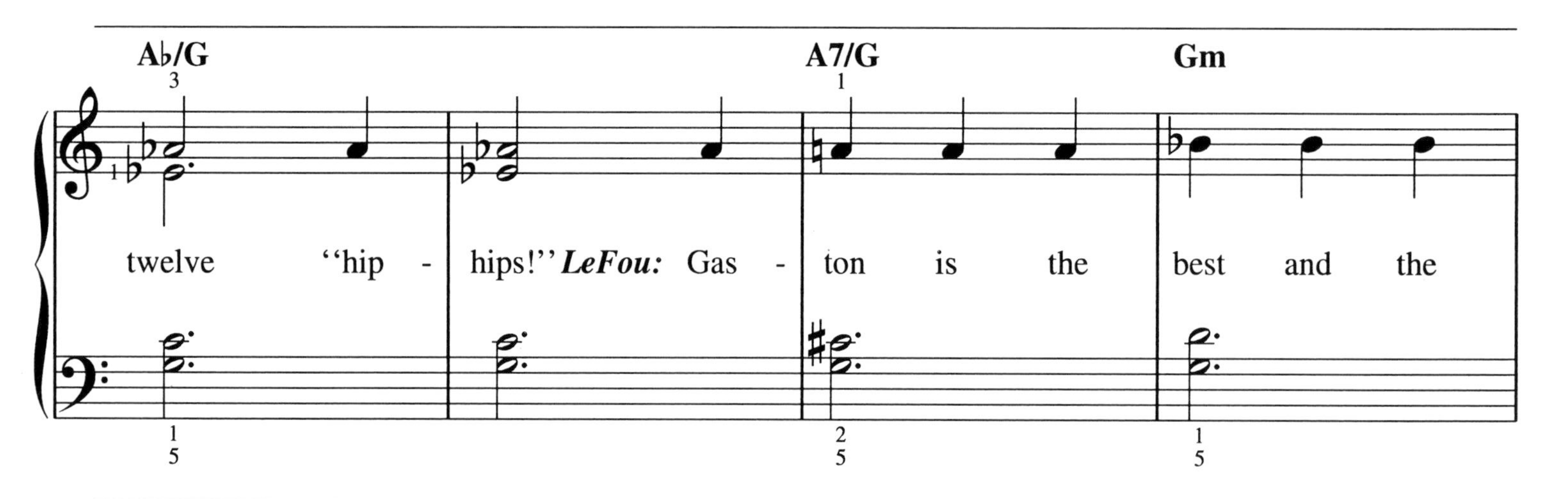
A♭/G
A7/G
Gm
twelve "hip - hips!" LeFou: Gas - ton is the best and the

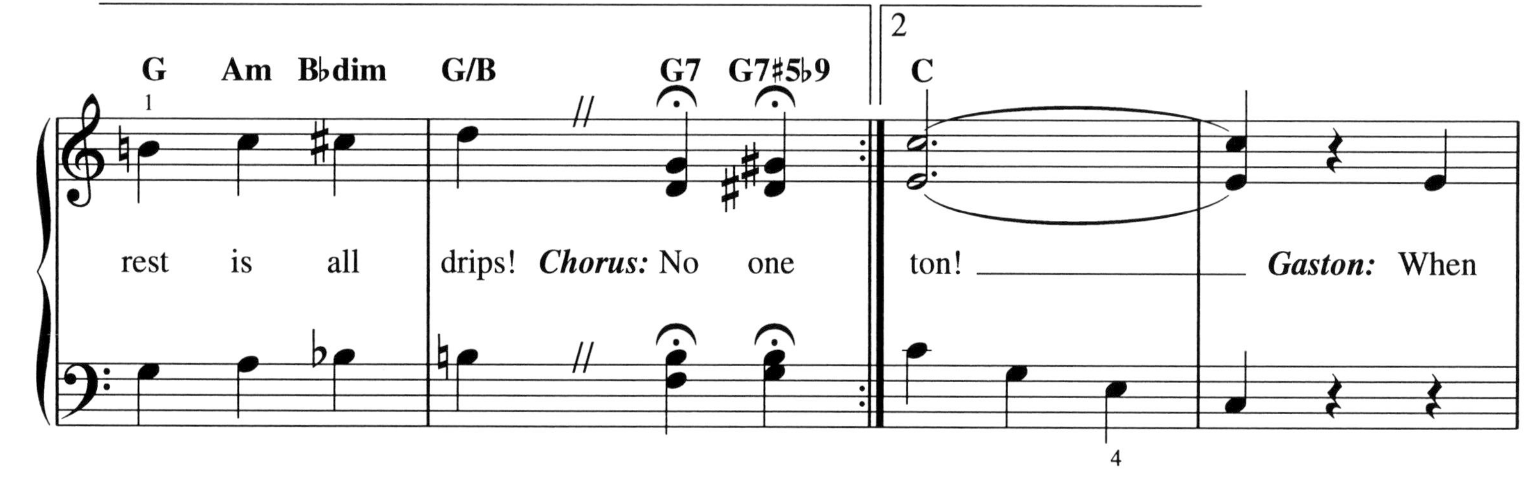
G Am B♭dim G/B G7 G7♯5♭9
2
C
rest is all drips! Chorus: No one ton! Gaston: When

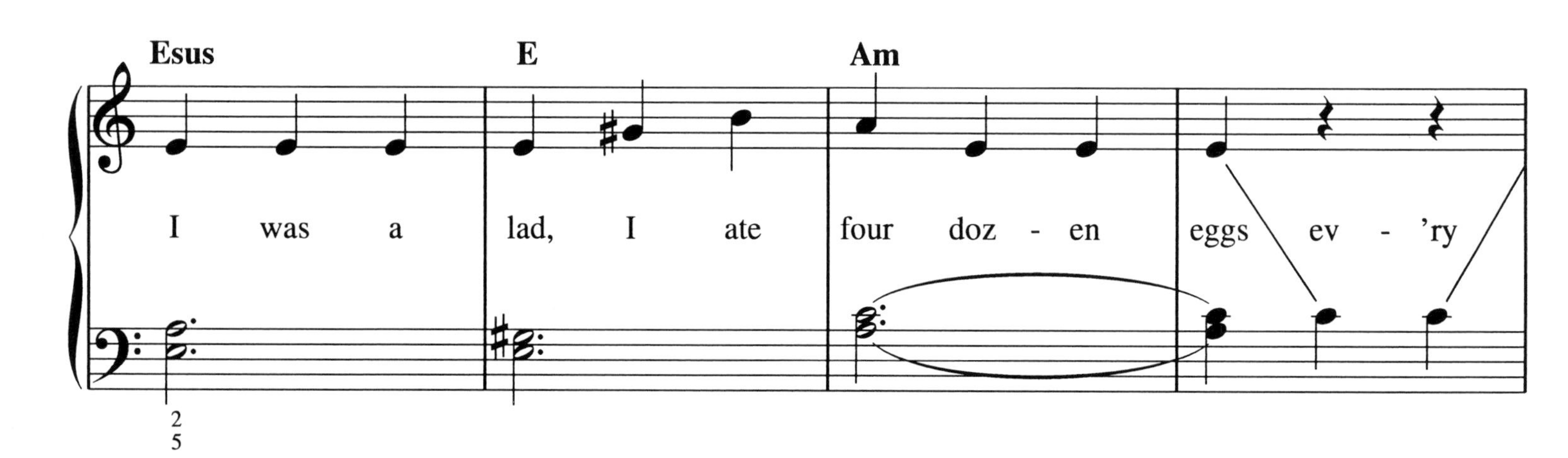
Esus
E
Am
I was a lad, I ate four doz - en eggs ev - 'ry

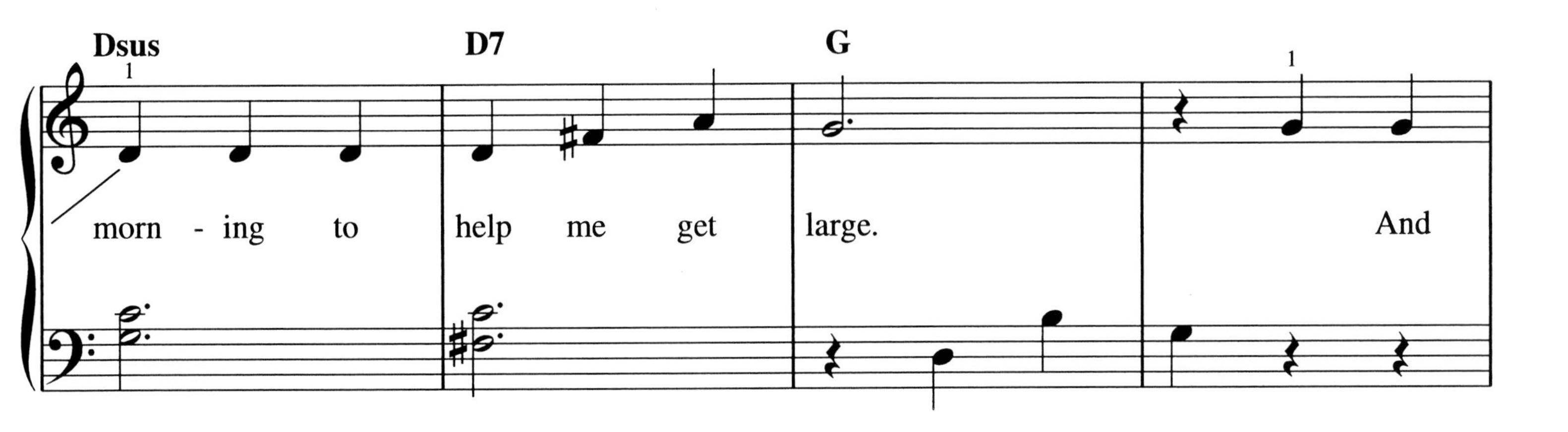
Dsus
D7
G
morn - ing to
help me get
large.
And

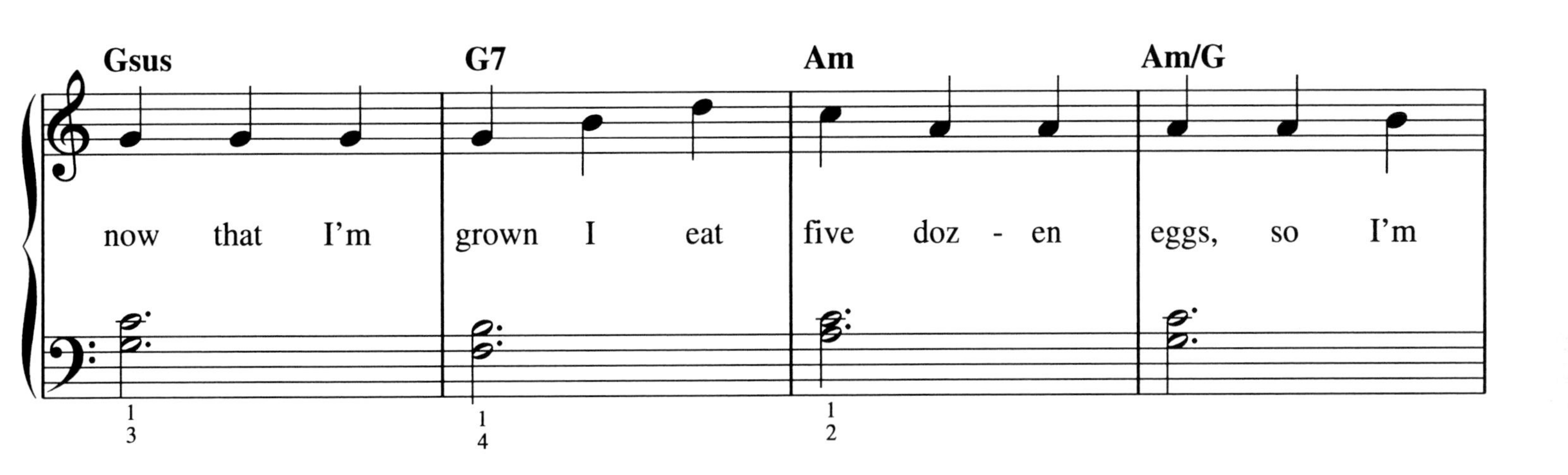
Gsus
G7
Am
Am/G
now that I'm
grown I eat
five doz - en
eggs, so I'm

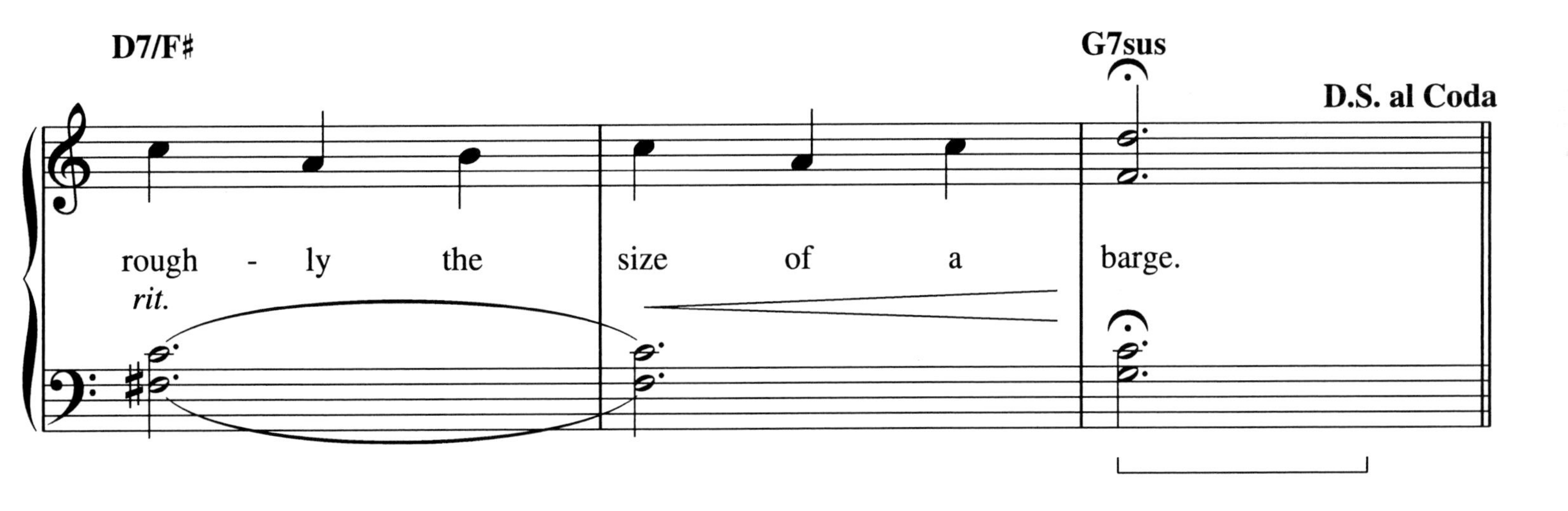
D7/F#
G7sus
D.S. al Coda
rough - ly the
size of a
barge.
rit.

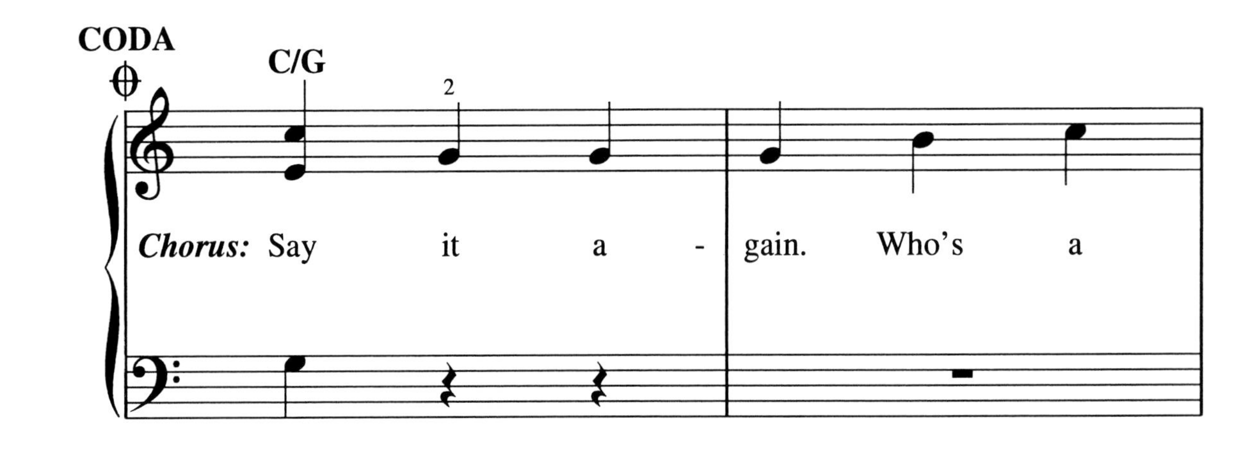
CODA
C/G
Chorus: Say it a - gain. Who's a

F♯m7♭5
C/G
3
2
1
2
man a - mong
men? And then
say it once
more. Who's the

A7
F
F♯dim
3
1
he - ro next
door? Who's a
su - per suc -
cess? Don't you

C/G
A7
F
E7
1
know? Can't you
guess? Ask his
fans and his
five hang - ers

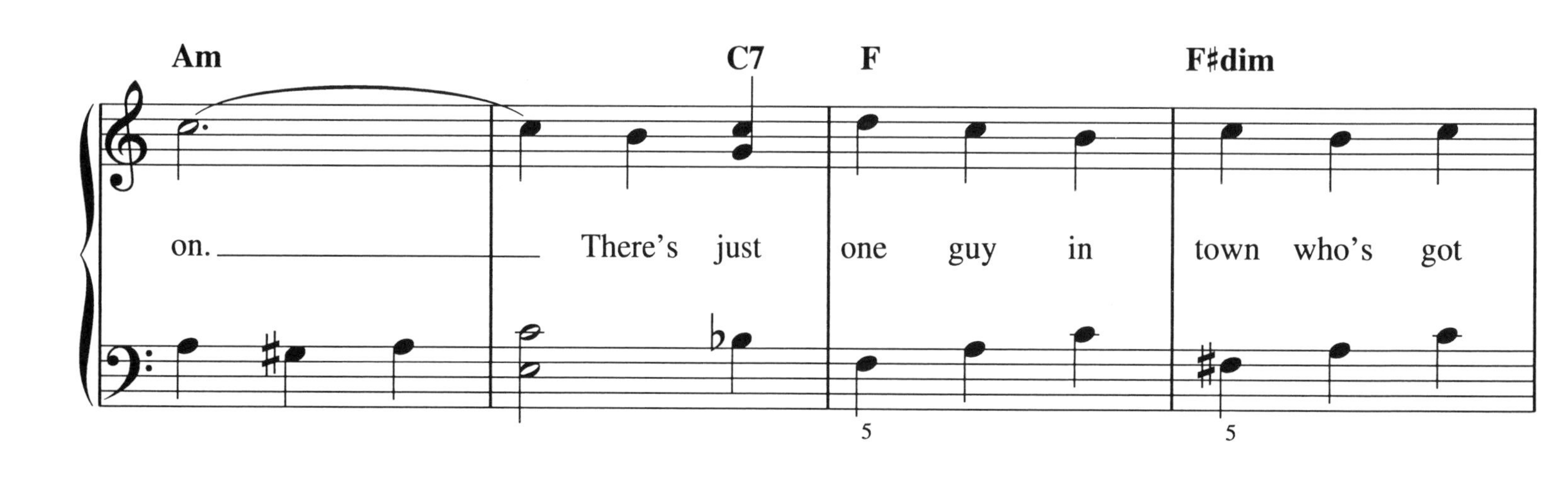
Am
C7
F
F♯dim
on.
There's just
one guy in
town who's got
5
5

C/G
A7
N.C.
Dm7
all of it down.
LeFou: And his name's G - A -

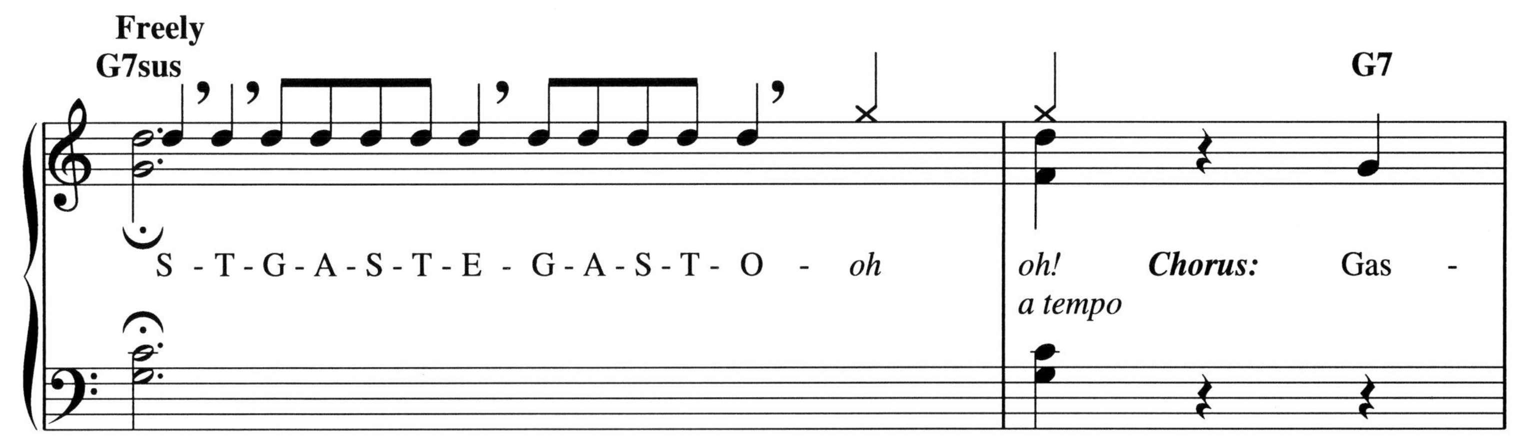
Freely
G7sus
G7
S - T - G - A - S - T - E - G - A - S - T - O - oh
oh! Chorus: Gas -
a tempo

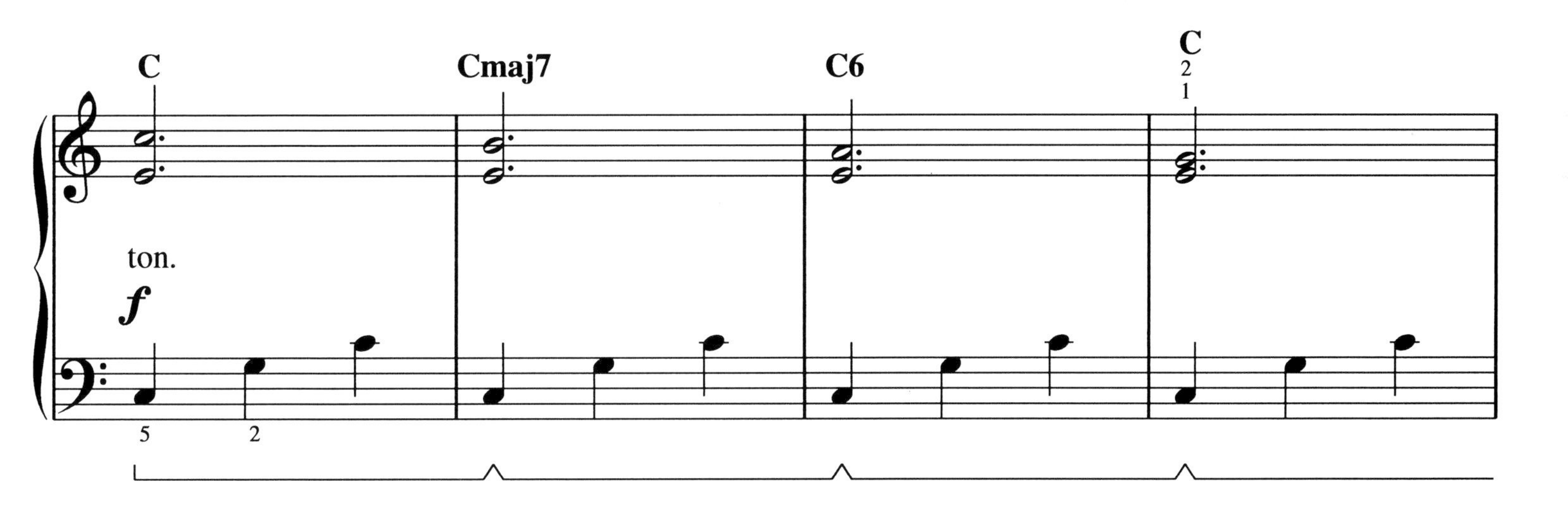
C
Cmaj7
C6
C
ton.
f

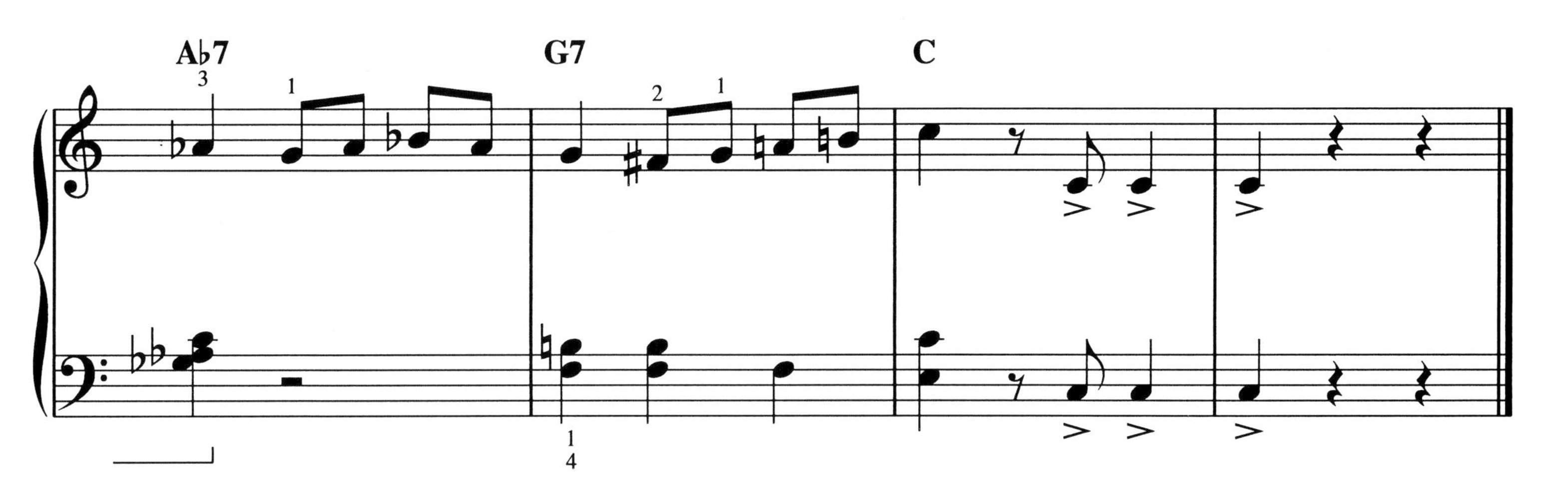
A♭7
G7
C

GASTON (REPRISE)

Lyrics by HOWARD ASHMAN
Music by ALAN MENKEN

Moderately Fast Waltz

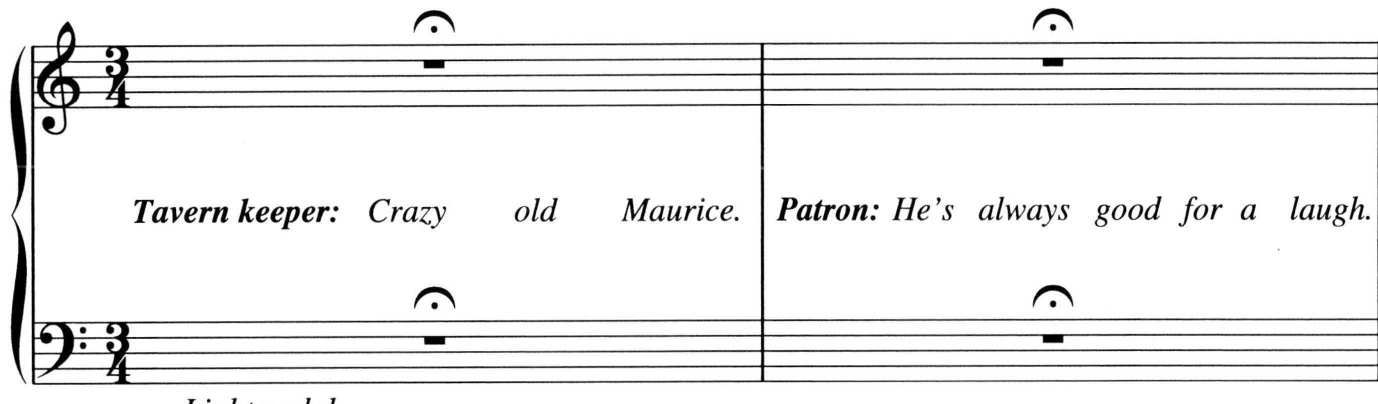

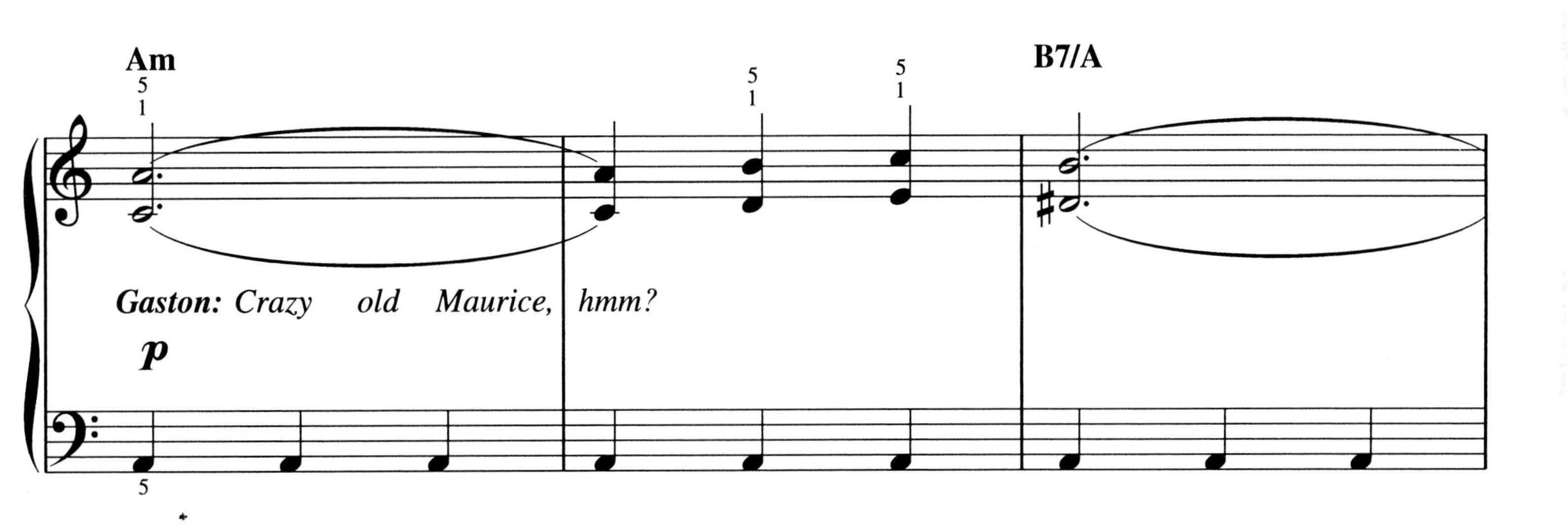

B7/A
mp
Gaston: Le - Fou, I'm a - fraid I've been think - ing.

Bdim/A
Am
LeFou: A dan - ger - ous pas - time. Gaston: I know.

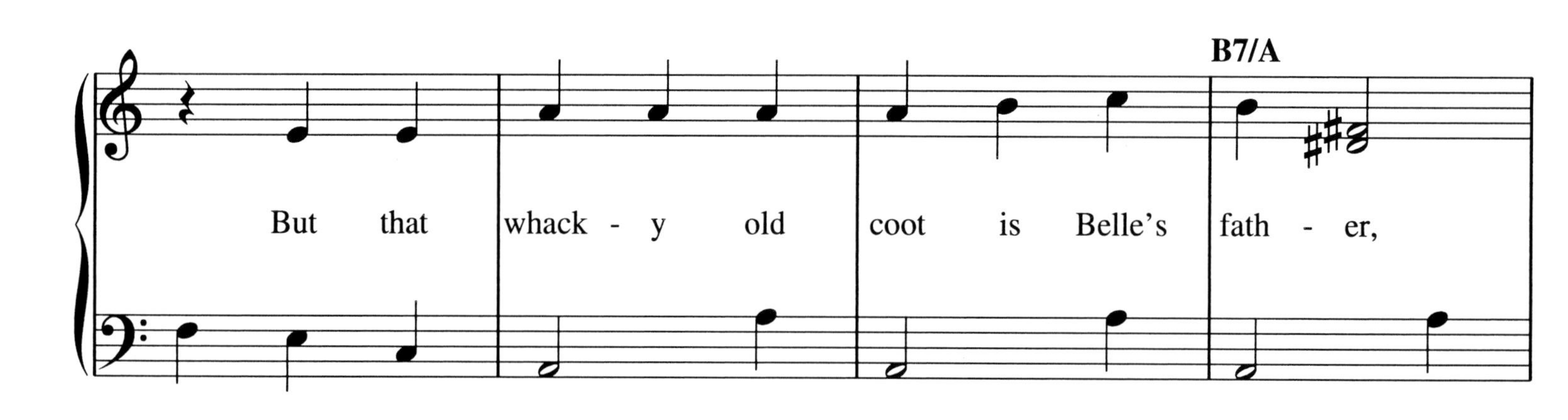
B7/A
But that whack - y old coot is Belle's fath - er,

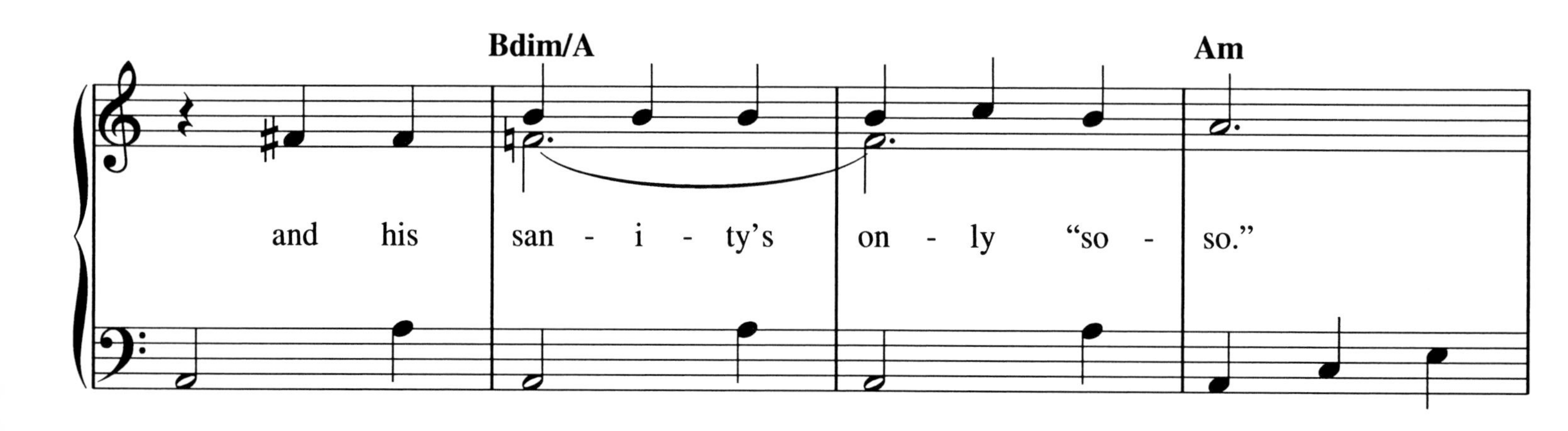
Bdim/A
Am
and his san - i - ty's on - ly "so - so."

C
D/C
Now the wheels in my head have been turn - ing

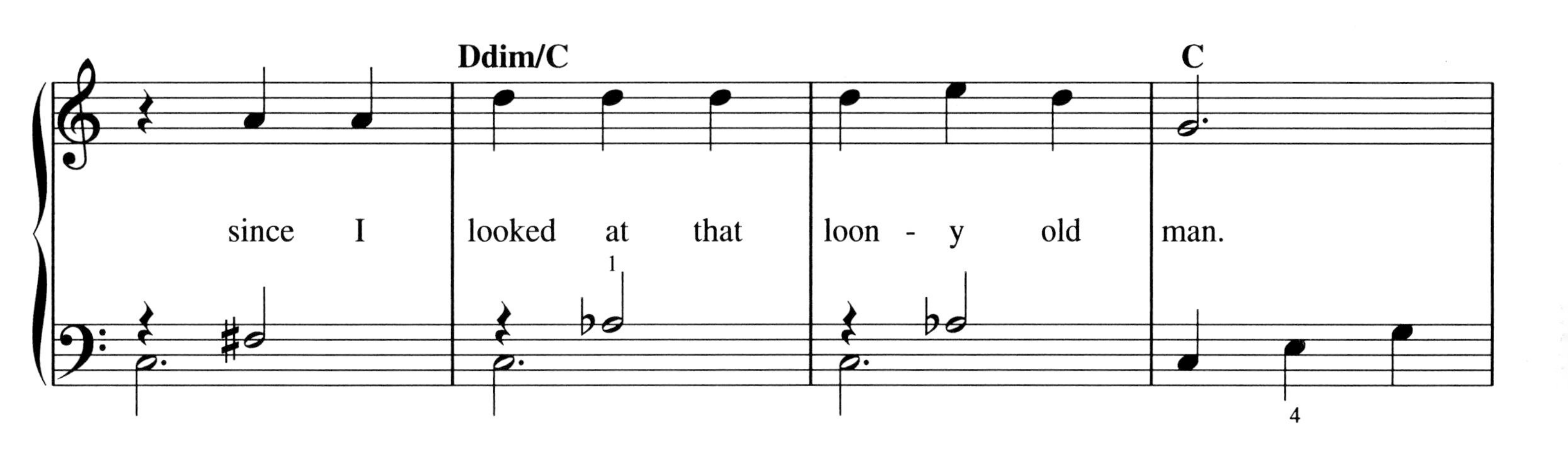
Ddim/C
C
since I looked at that loon - y old man.

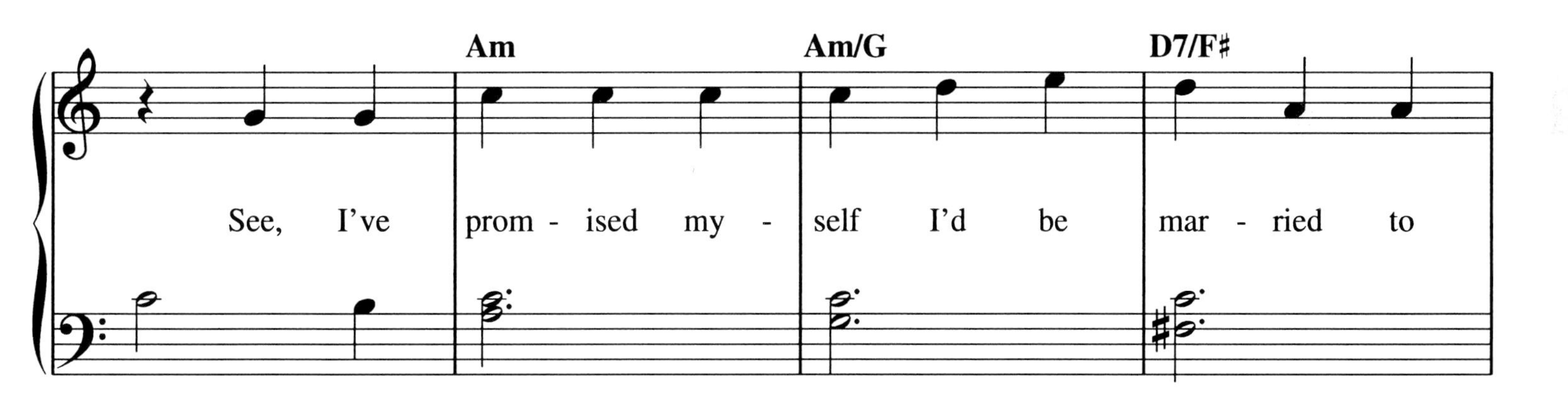
Am
Am/G
D7/F♯
See, I've prom - ised my - self I'd be mar - ried to

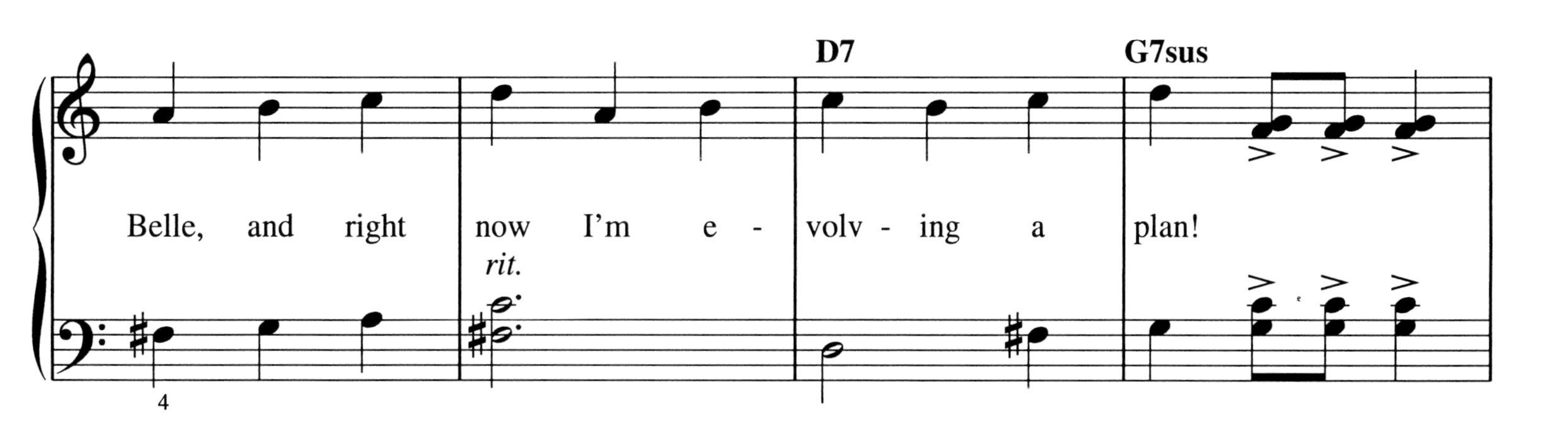
D7
G7sus
Belle, and right now I'm e - volv - ing a plan!
rit.

G7
A♭7/G
p
If I.....
(whisper) LeFou:
a tempo
Yes? Gaston: Then we.....
(whisper) LeFou:

Cdim/G
G7
No! Would she....
Gaston: (whisper)
Guess! LeFou: Now I
get it! Both: Let's
rit.

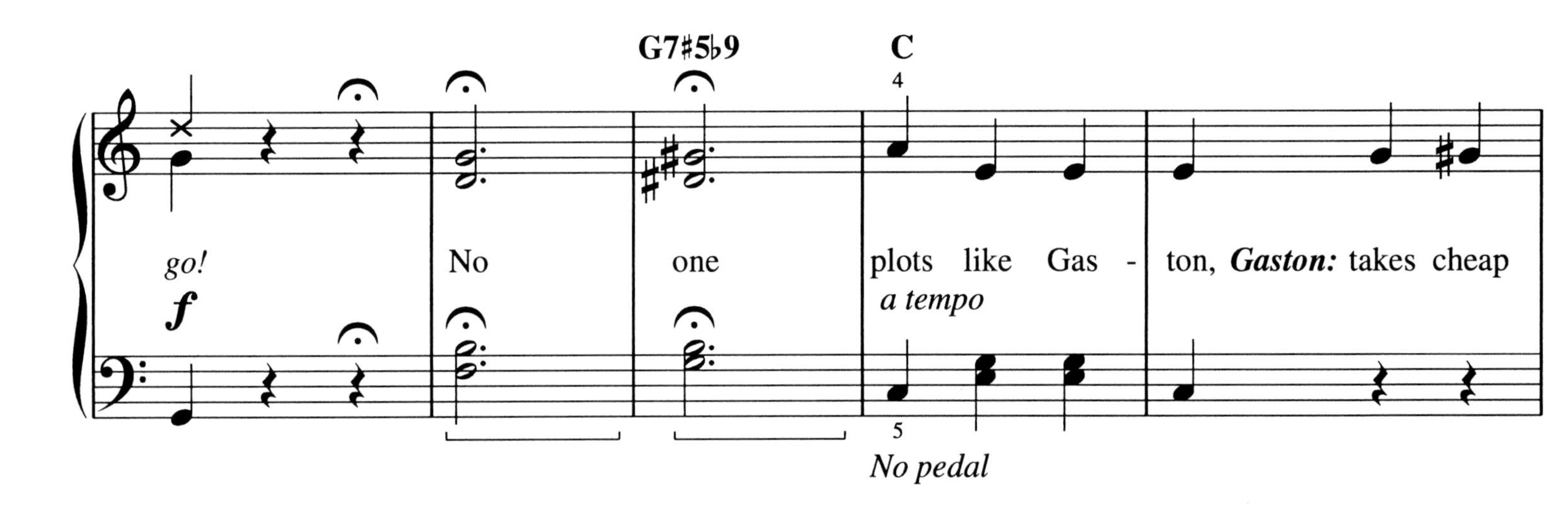
G7♯5♭9
C
go!
f
No one
plots like Gas - ton, Gaston: takes cheap
a tempo
No pedal

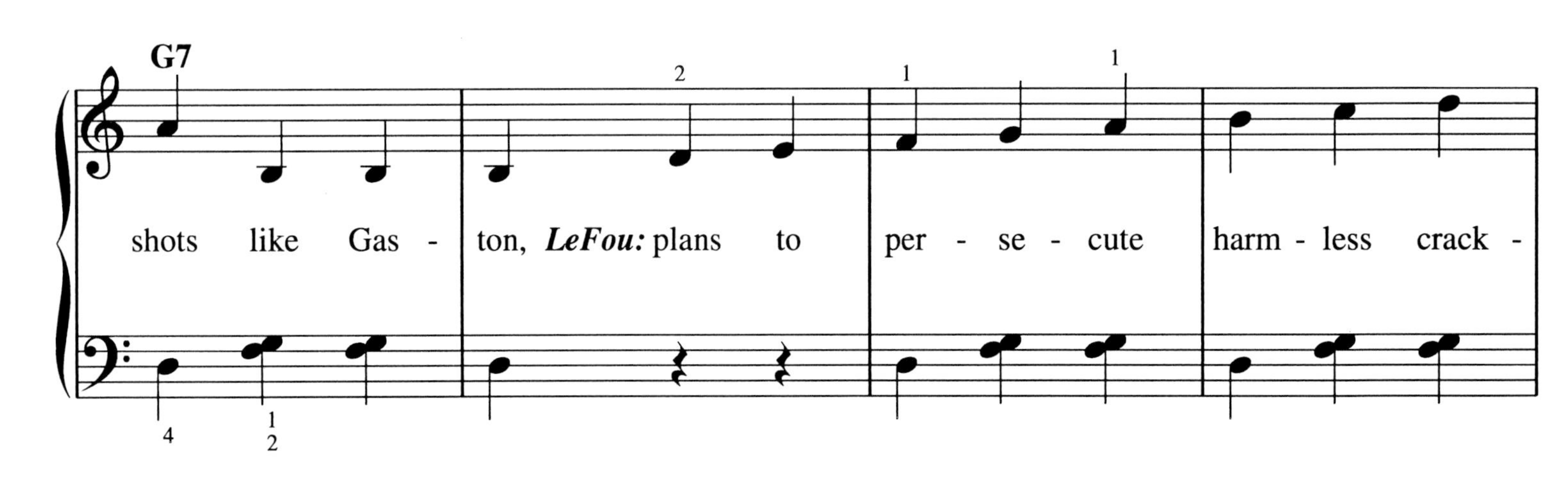
G7
shots like Gas - ton, LeFou: plans to per - se - cute harm - less crack -

C
Am
pots like Gas - ton. Chorus: So his mar - riage we soon - 'll be
1
2

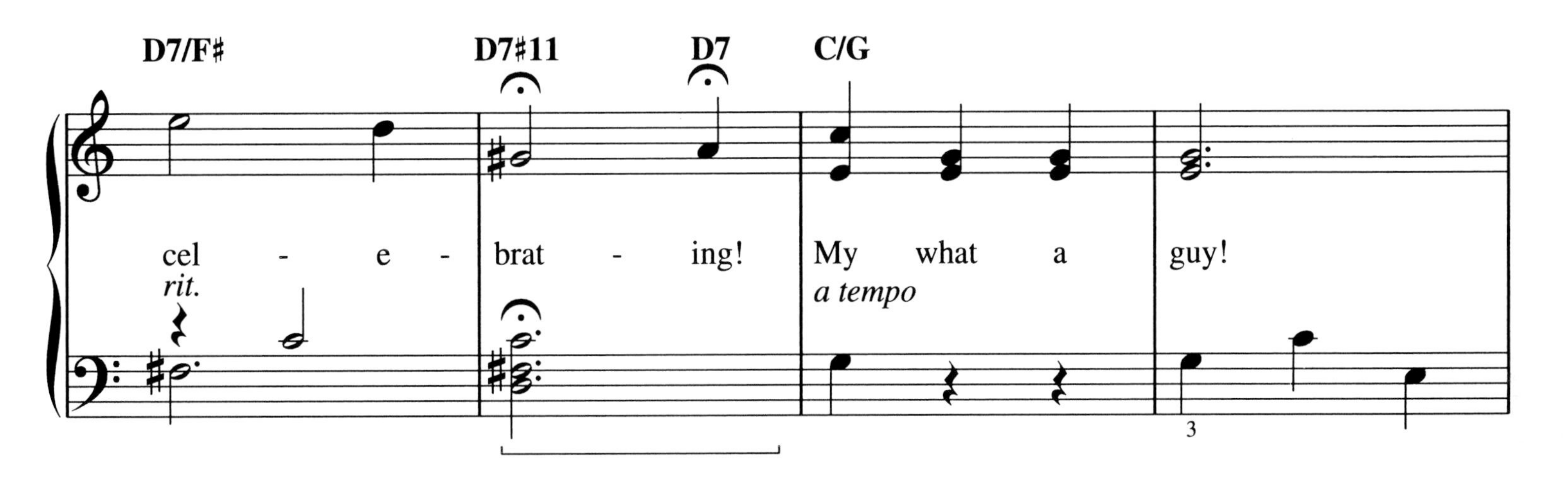
D7/F#
D7#11
D7
C/G
cel - e - brat - ing! My what a guy!
rit.
a tempo
3

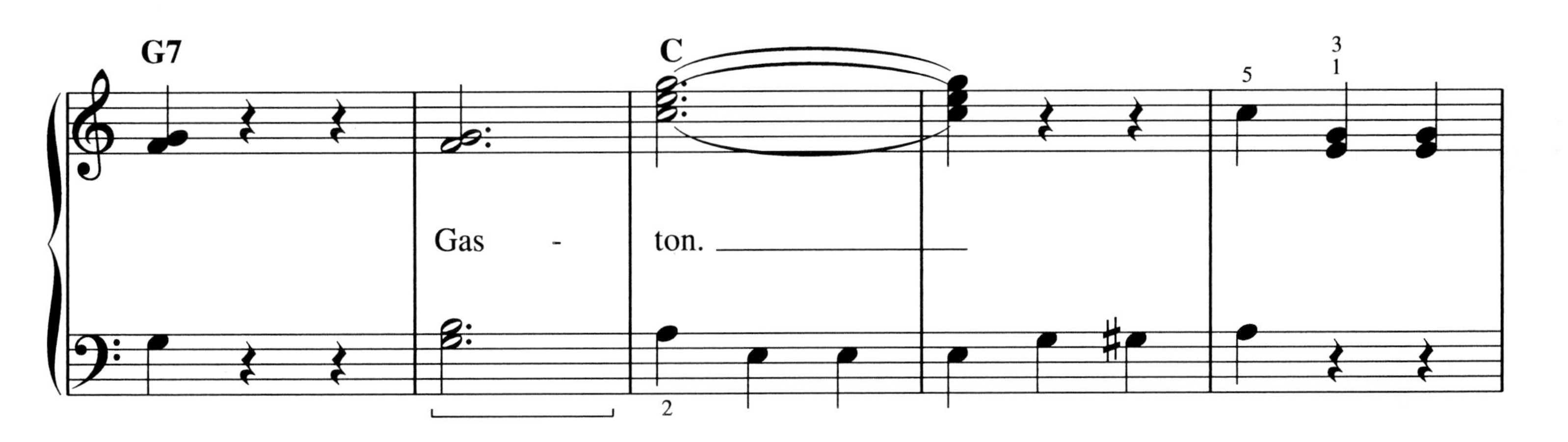
G7
C
5
3
1
Gas - ton.
2

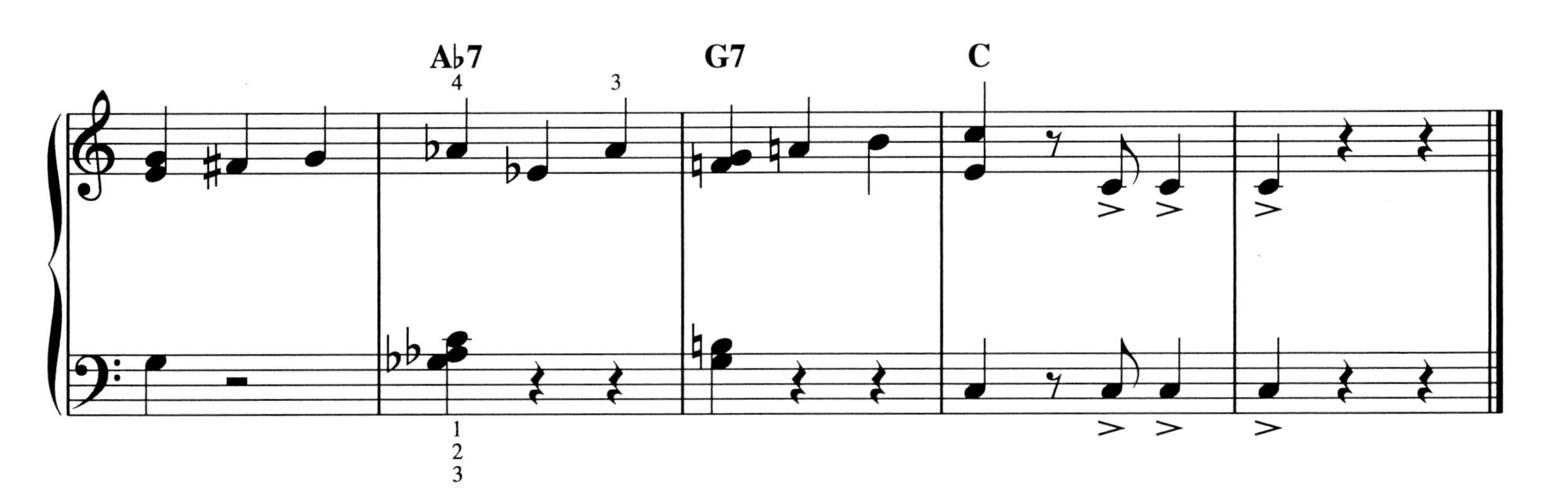
A♭7
4
3
G7
C
1
2
3

BE OUR GUEST

Lyrics by HOWARD ASHMAN
Music by ALAN MENKEN

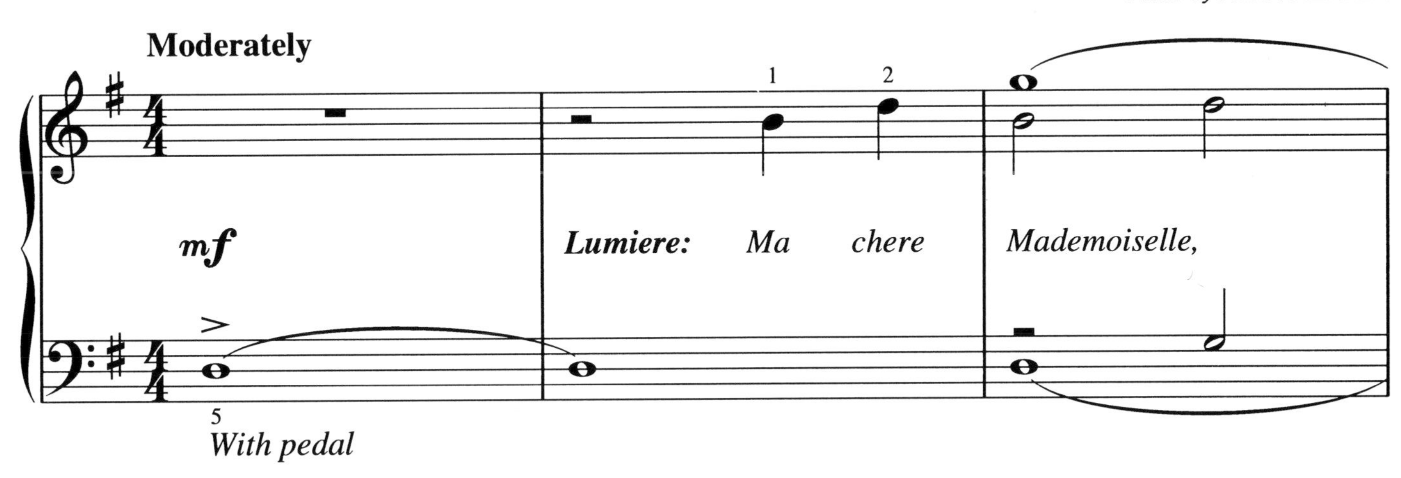

N.C.
G
Gmaj7
your dinner!
Be our
guest! Be our
guest! Put our
a tempo
No pedal

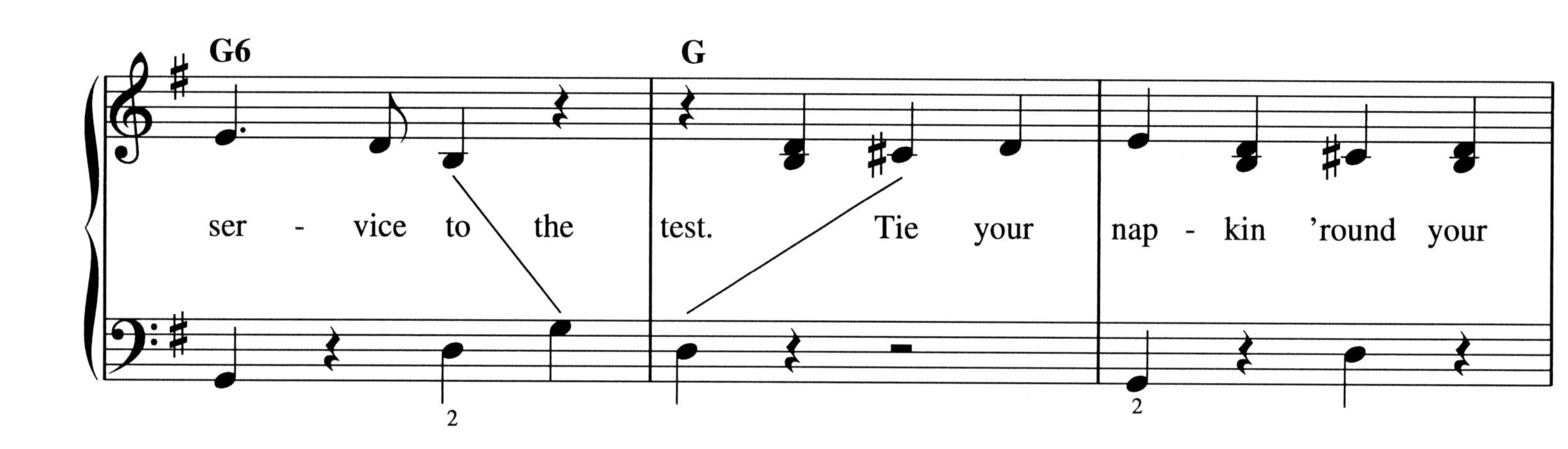
G6
G
ser - vice to the
test. Tie your
nap - kin 'round your

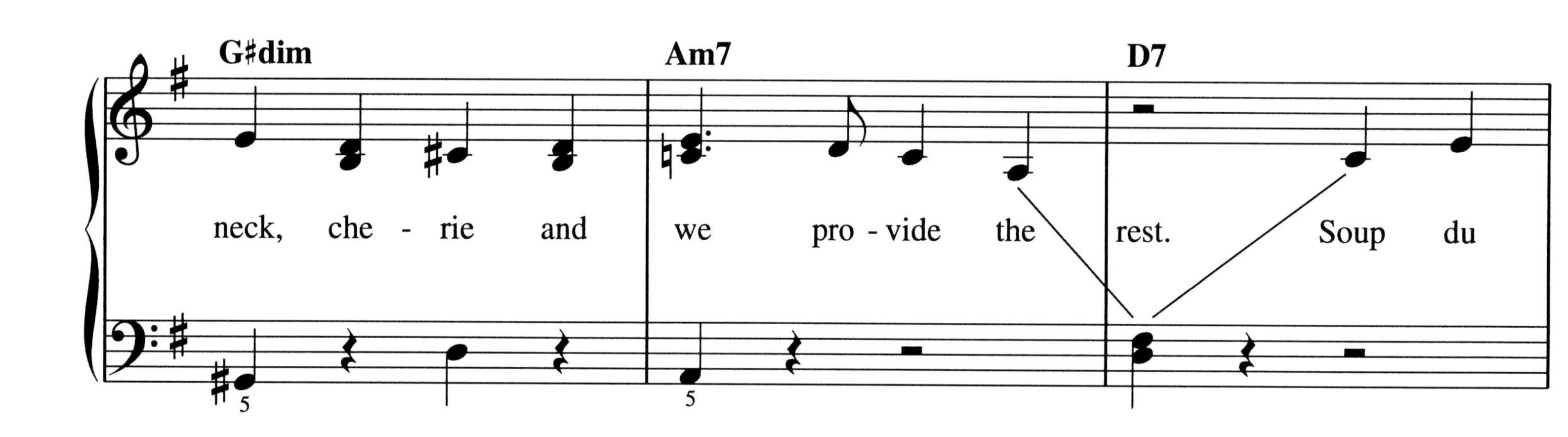
G♯dim
Am7
D7
neck, che - rie and
we pro - vide the
rest. Soup du

Am
Am♯7
Am7
jour! Hot hors
d'oeuvres! Why, we
on - ly live to

D7
Am7
B♭dim
serve. Try the grey stuff, it's de - li - cious! Don't be -

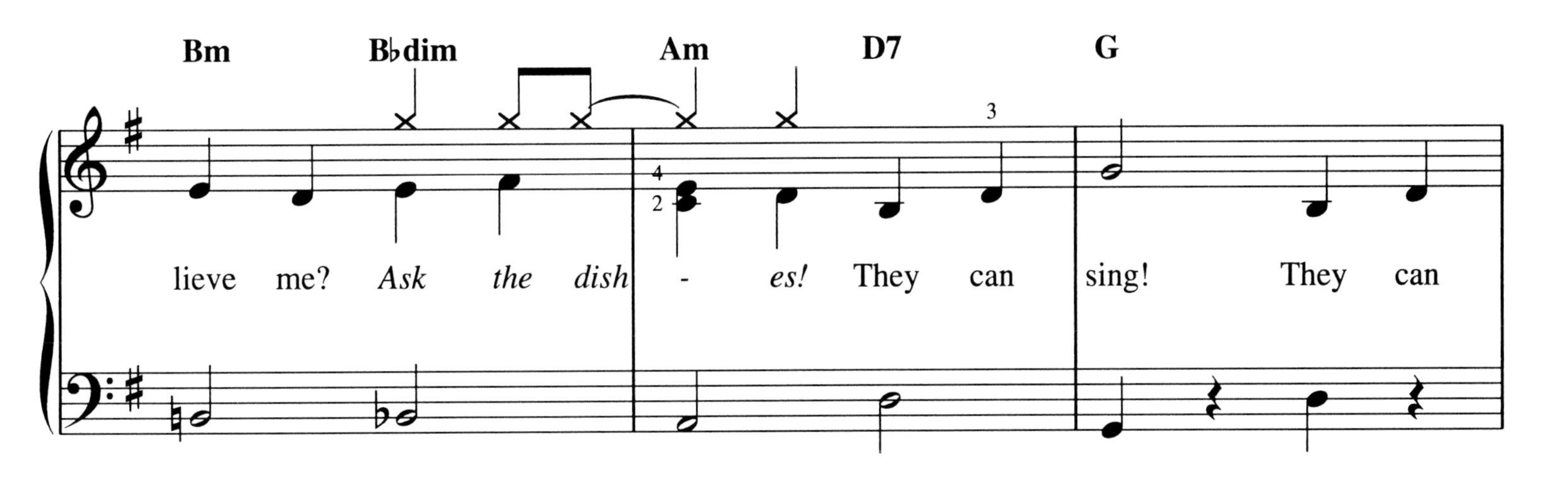
Bm
B♭dim
Am
D7
G
lieve me? Ask the dish - es! They can sing! They can

Gmaj7
G6
G
dance! Af - ter all, Miss, this is France! And a

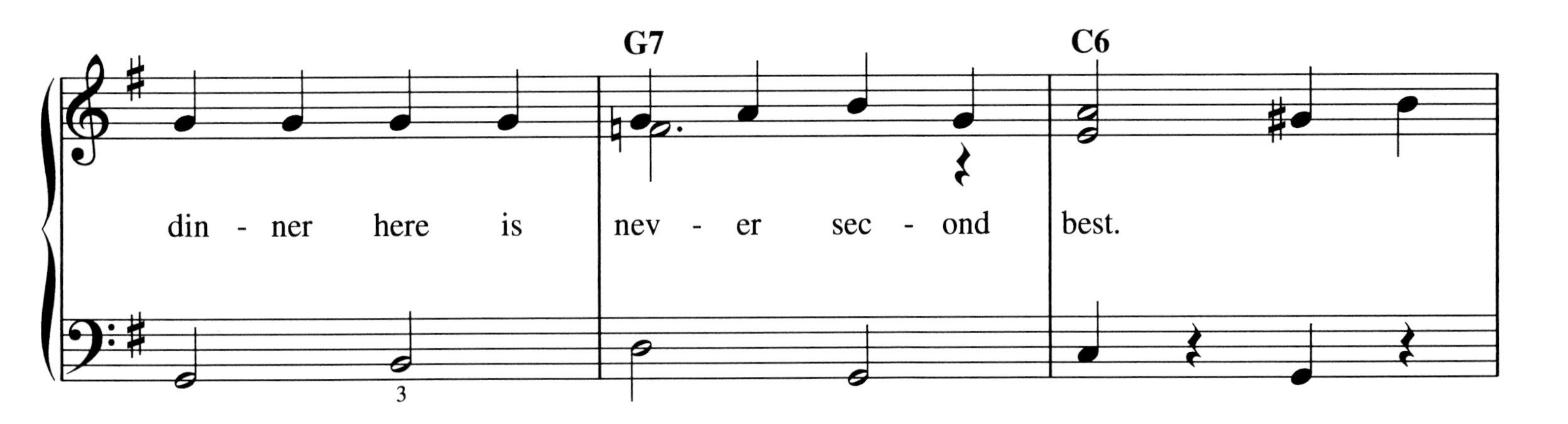
G7
C6
din - ner here is nev - er sec - ond best.

B
C#m
Ddim
B7/D#
Go on, un - fold your men - u, take a

Em
A7
Am
glance, and then you'll be our guest, oui, our

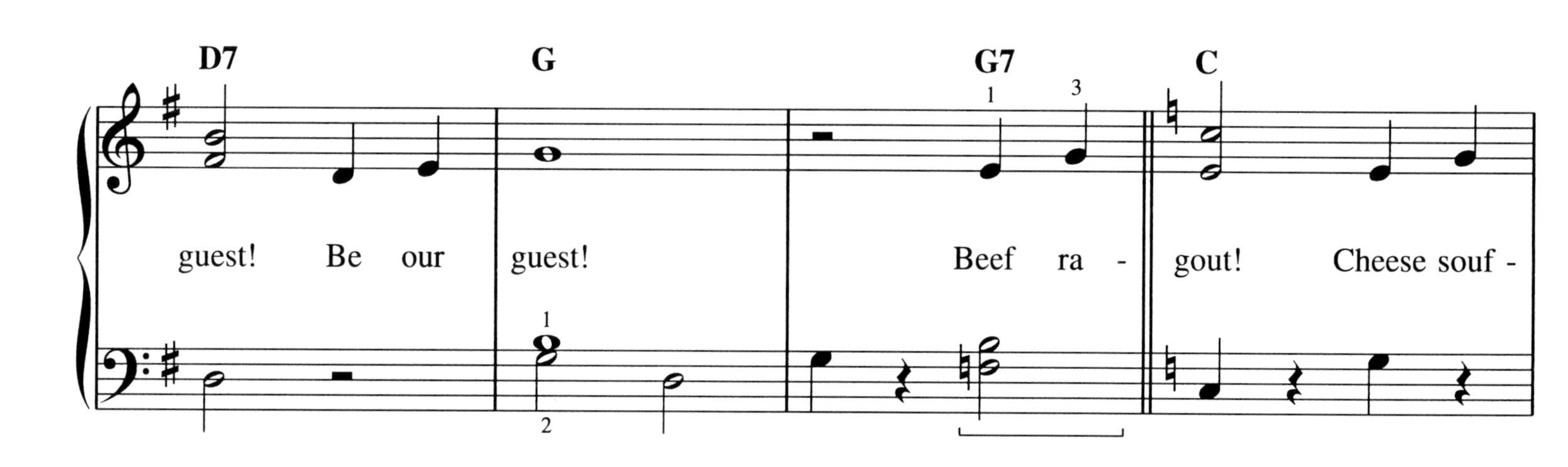
D7
G
G7
C
guest! Be our guest! Beef ra - gout! Cheese souf -

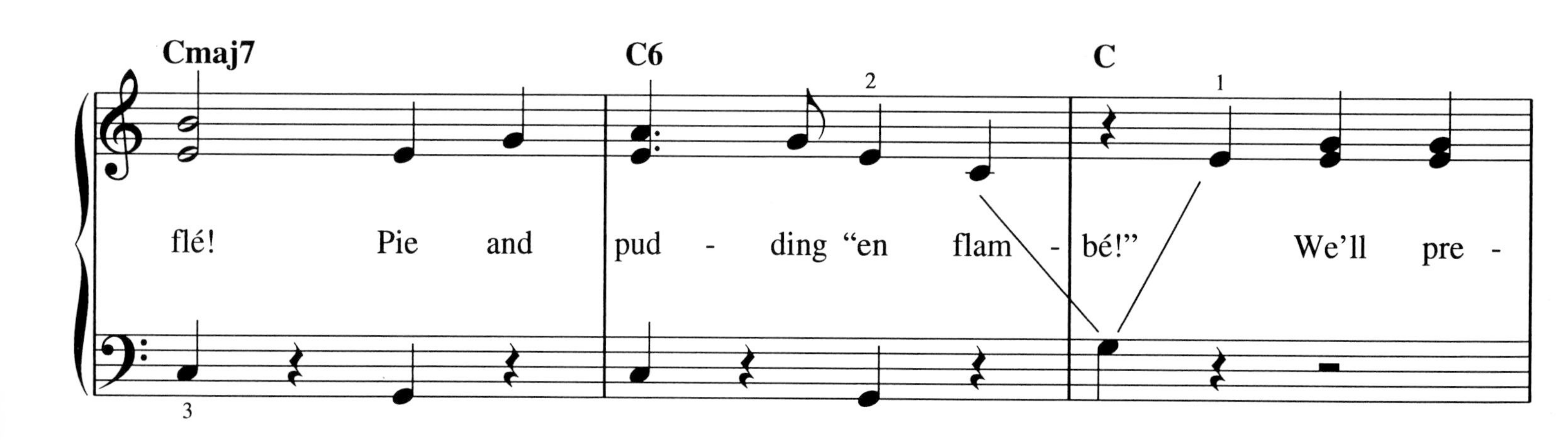
Cmaj7
C6
C
flé! Pie and pud - ding "en flam - bé!" We'll pre -

C♯dim
Dm7
pare and serve with flair a cu - li - na - ry ca - ba -
5
5
5

G7
Dm
Dm♯7
3
1
ret! You're a - lone and you're scared but the

Dm7
G
Dm7
2
ban - quet's all pre - pared. No one's gloom - y or com -

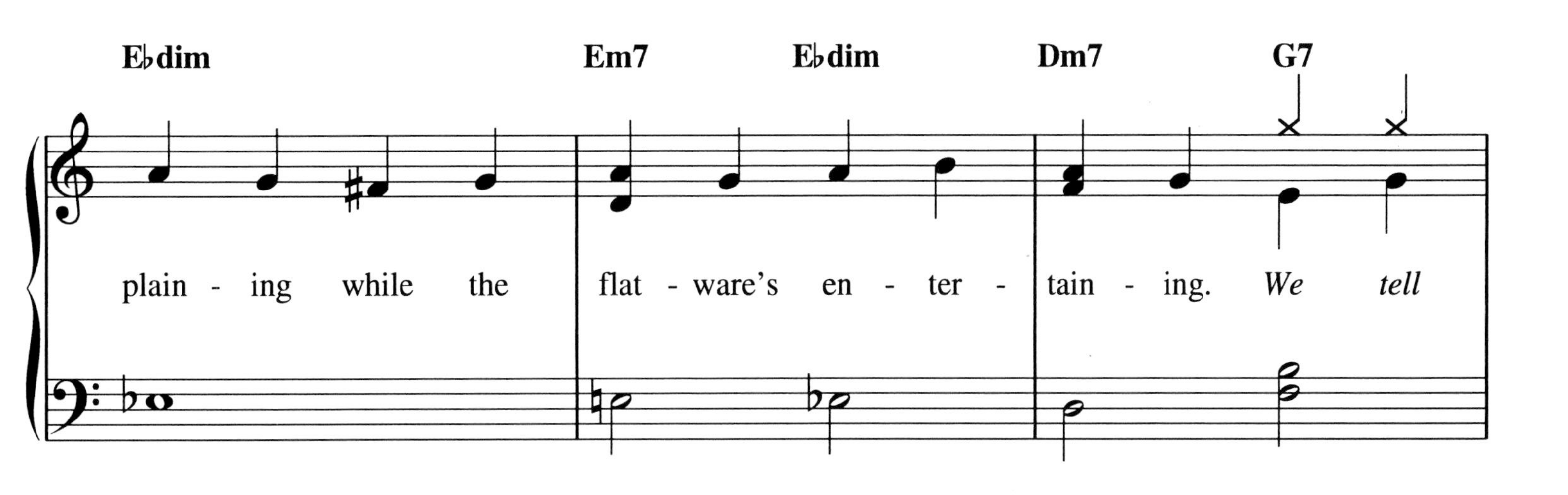
E♭dim
Em7
E♭dim
Dm7
G7
plain - ing while the flat - ware's en - ter - tain - ing. We tell

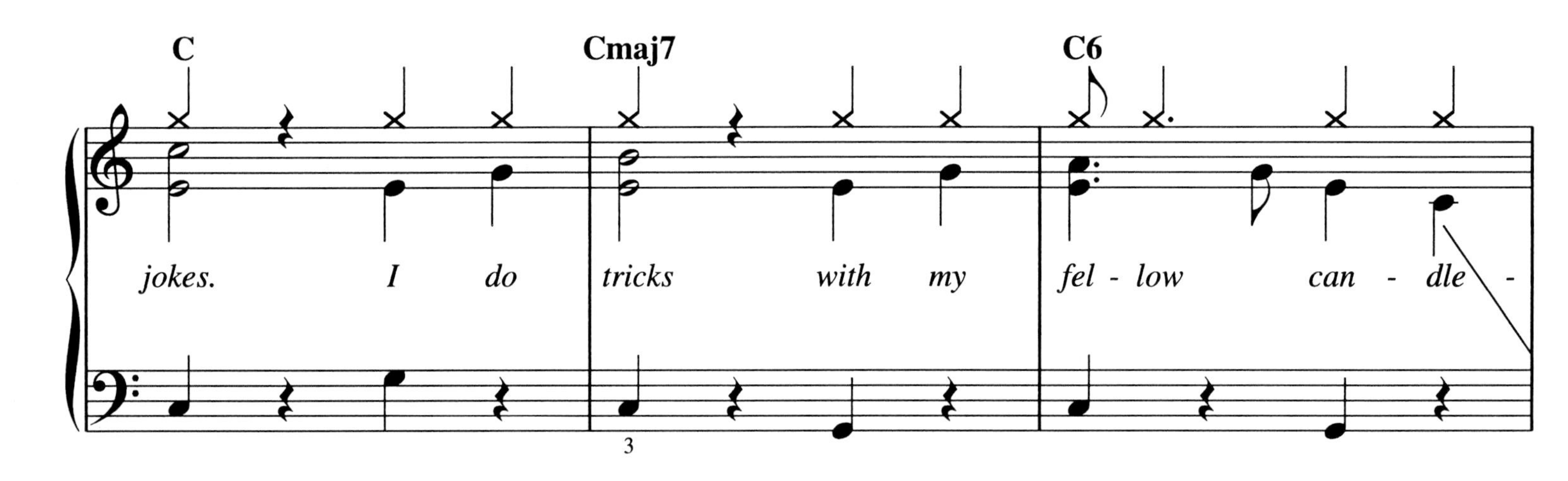
C
Cmaj7
C6
jokes. I do tricks with my fel - low can - dle -

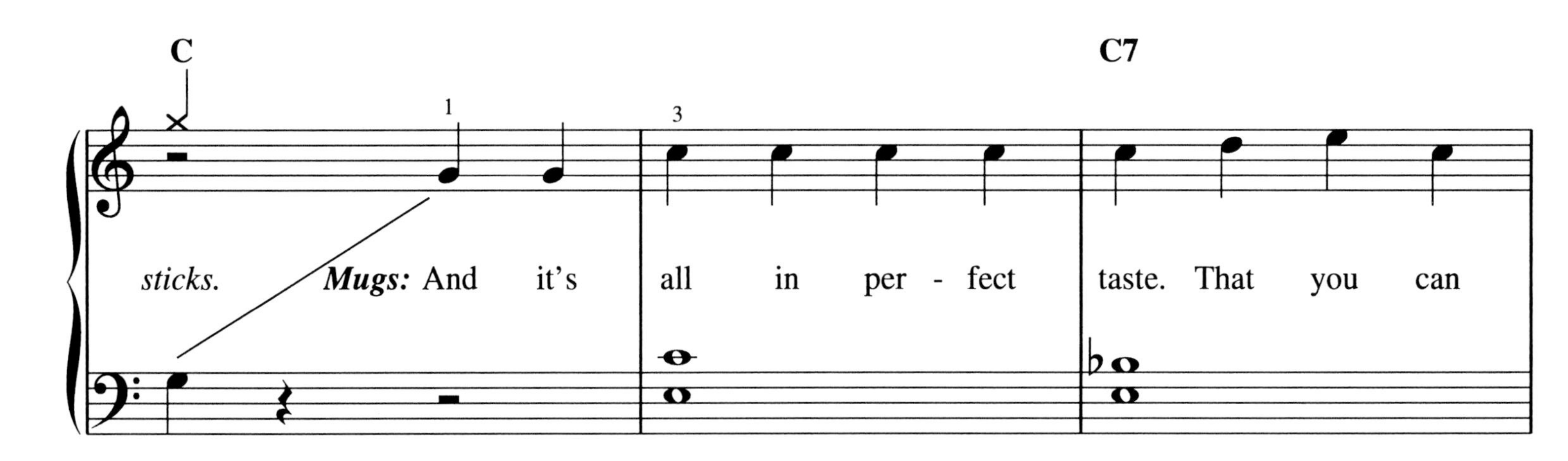
C
C7
sticks. Mugs: And it's all in per - fect taste. That you can

F6
E
F♯m7
Gdim
bet! All: Come on and lift your glass

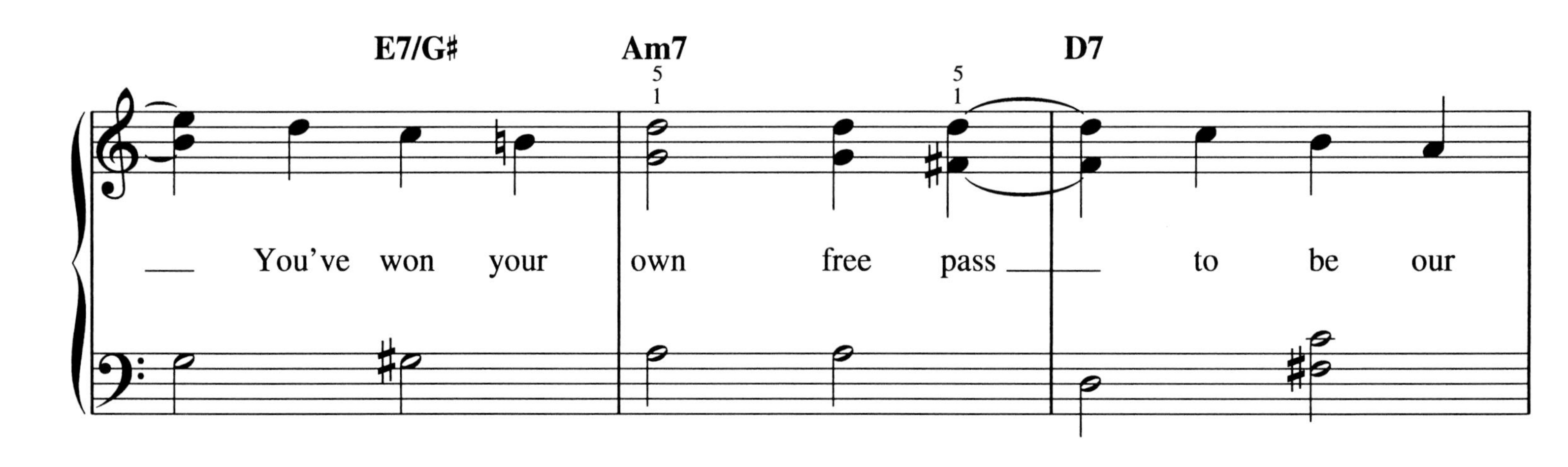
E7/G♯
Am7
D7
You've won your own free pass to be our

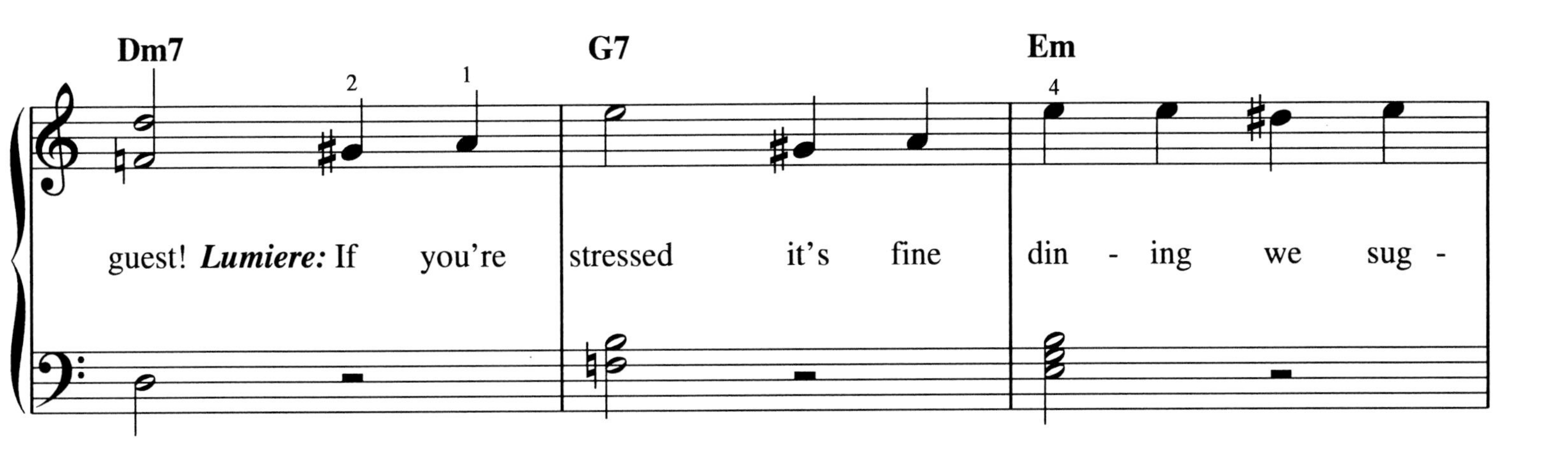
Dm7
G7
Em
guest! Lumiere: If you're stressed it's fine din - ing we sug -

A7♯5
Dm7
G7
C
gest. All: Be our guest! Be our guest! Be our guest!

E
Slower
Am
Lumiere:
mp
Freely
Life is so un - nerv - ing for a

E/G♯
Gdim
ser - vant who's not serv - ing. He's not whole with - out a

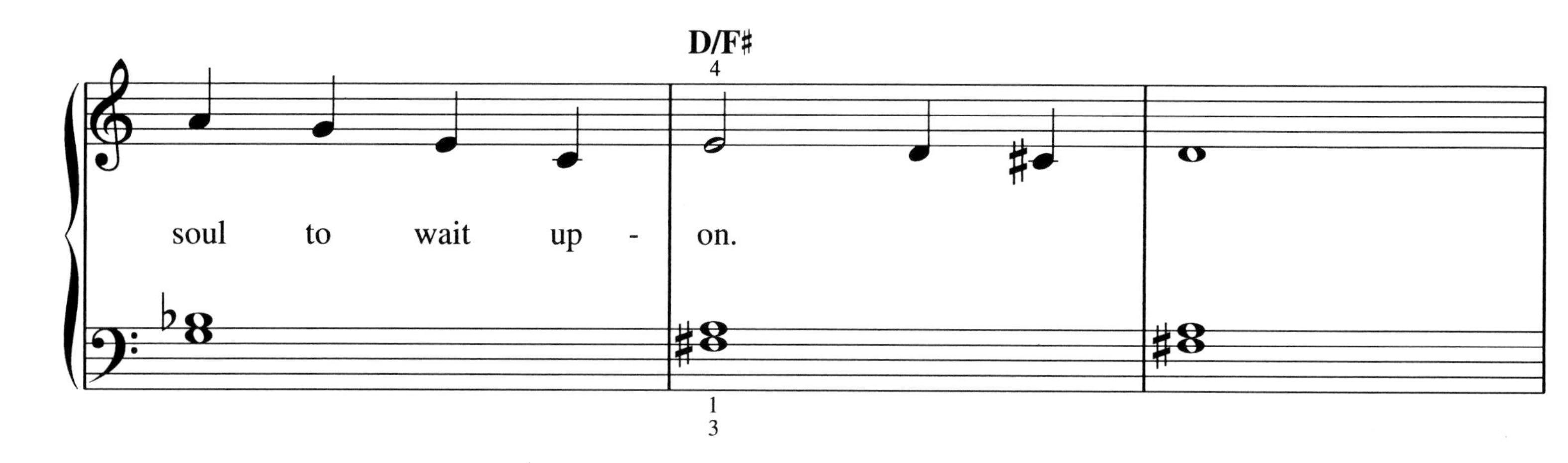
D/F♯
soul to wait up - on.

Fdim
Em
Ah, those good old days when we were use - ful.

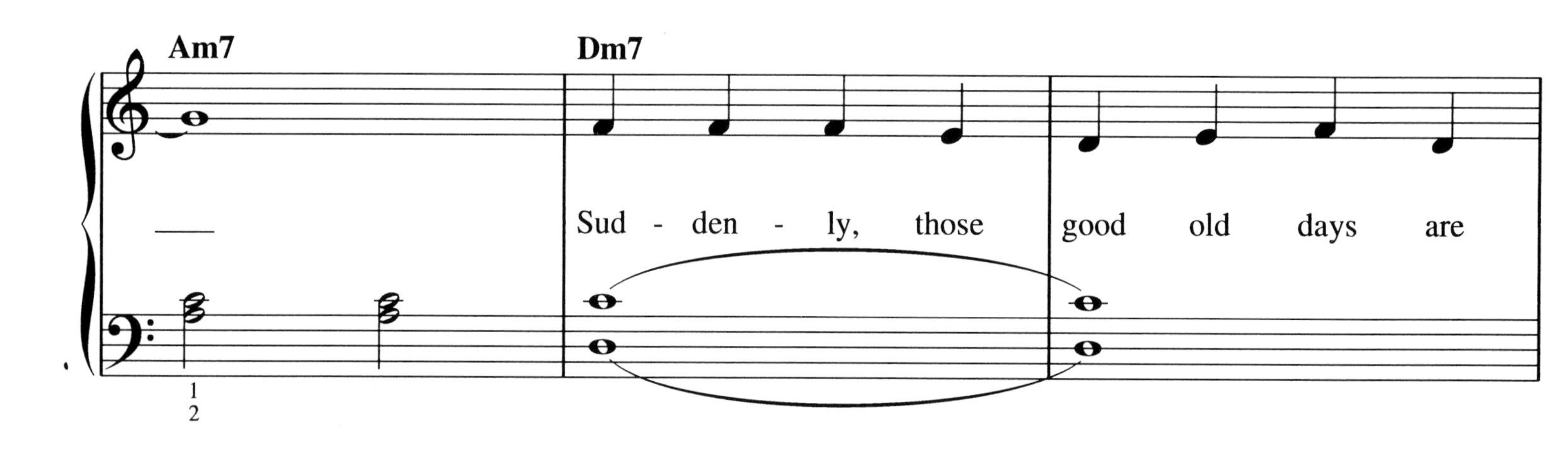
Am7
Dm7
Sud - den - ly, those good old days are

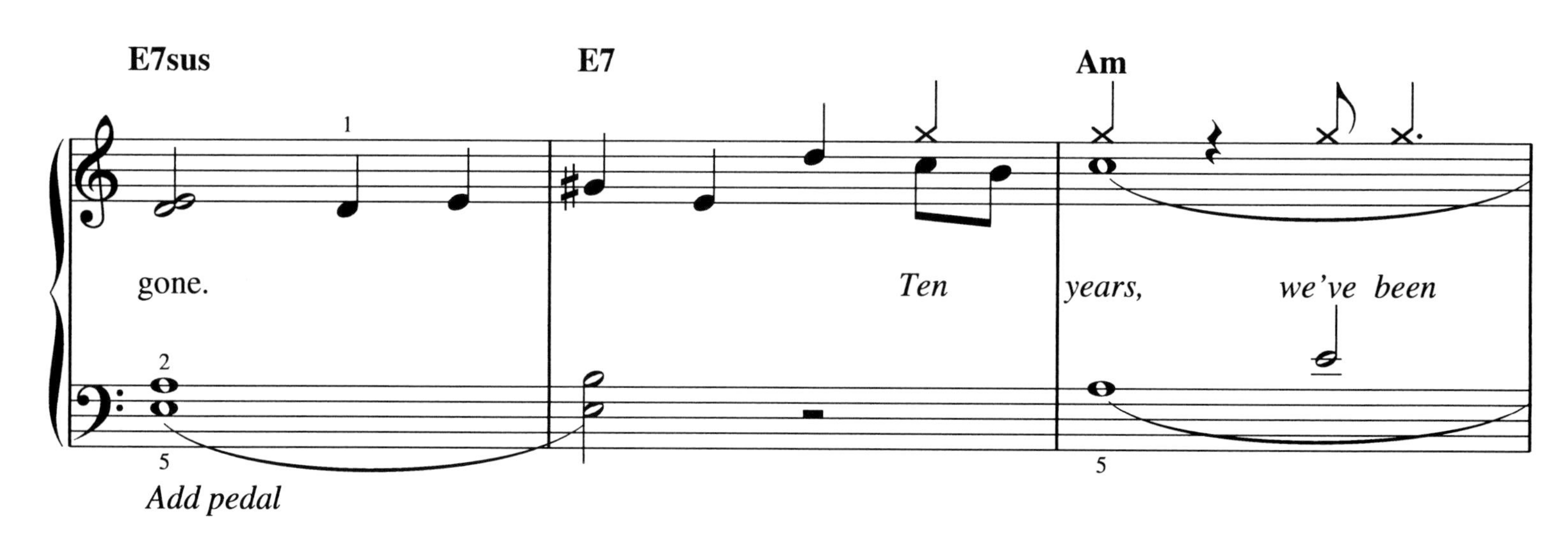
E7sus
E7
Am
gone.
Ten years, we've been
Add pedal

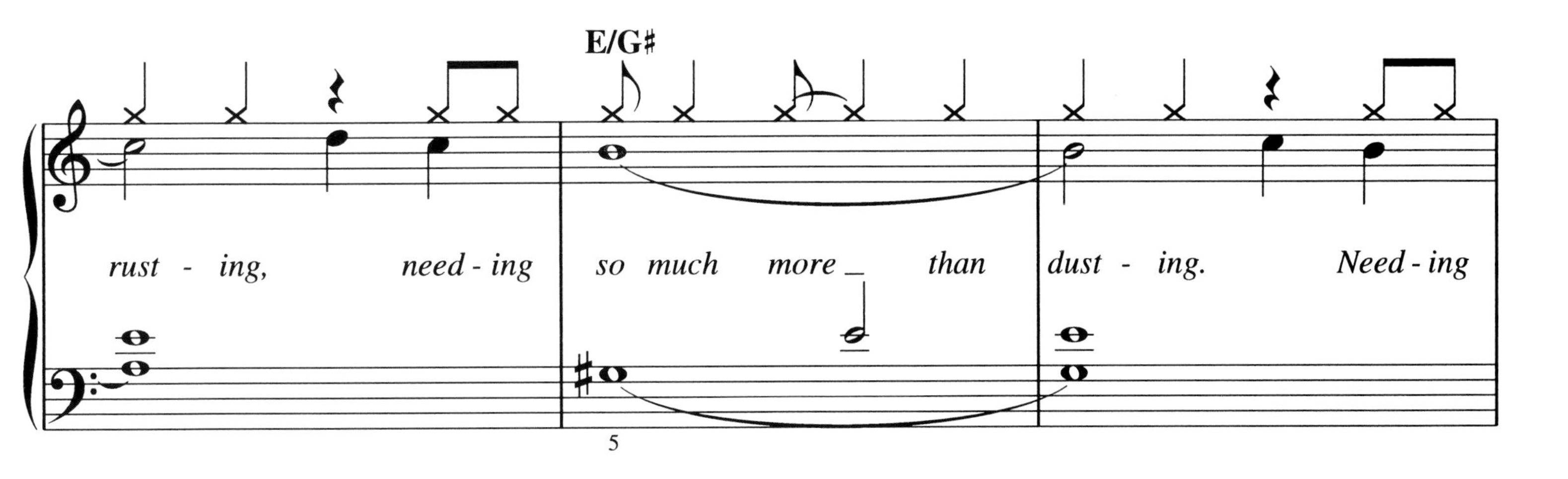
E/G♯
rust - ing, need - ing so much more _ than dust - ing. Need - ing
5

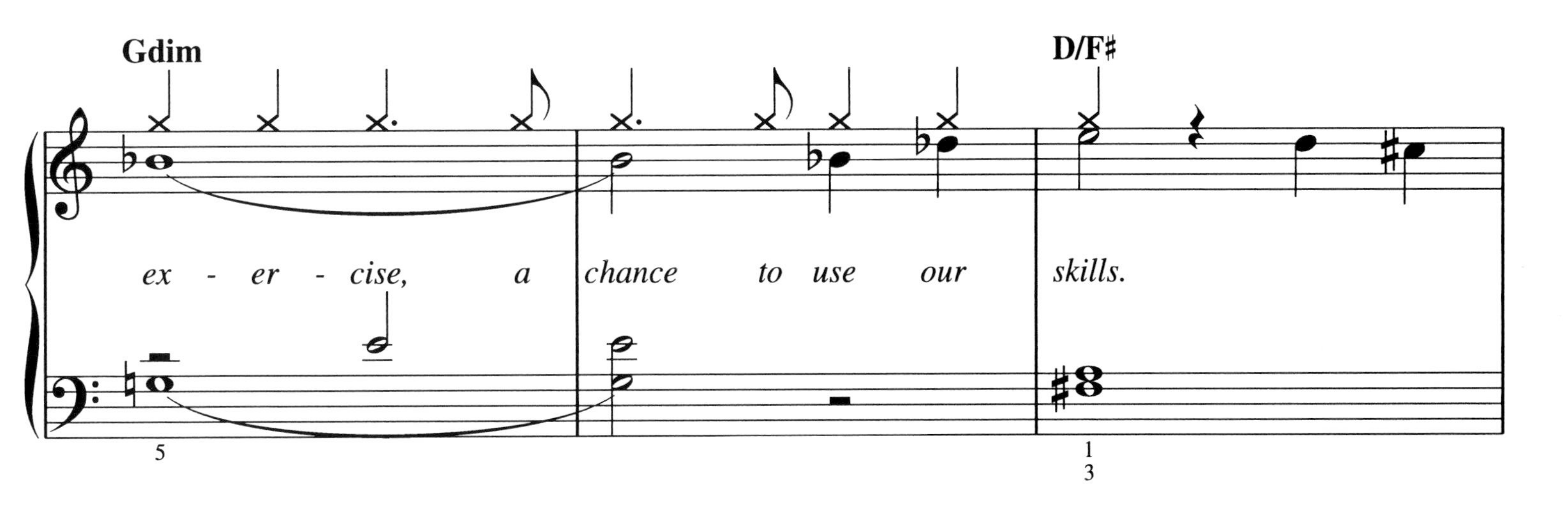
Gdim
D/F♯
ex - er - cise, a chance to use our skills.
5
1
3

Fdim
3
Most days, we just lay a - round the

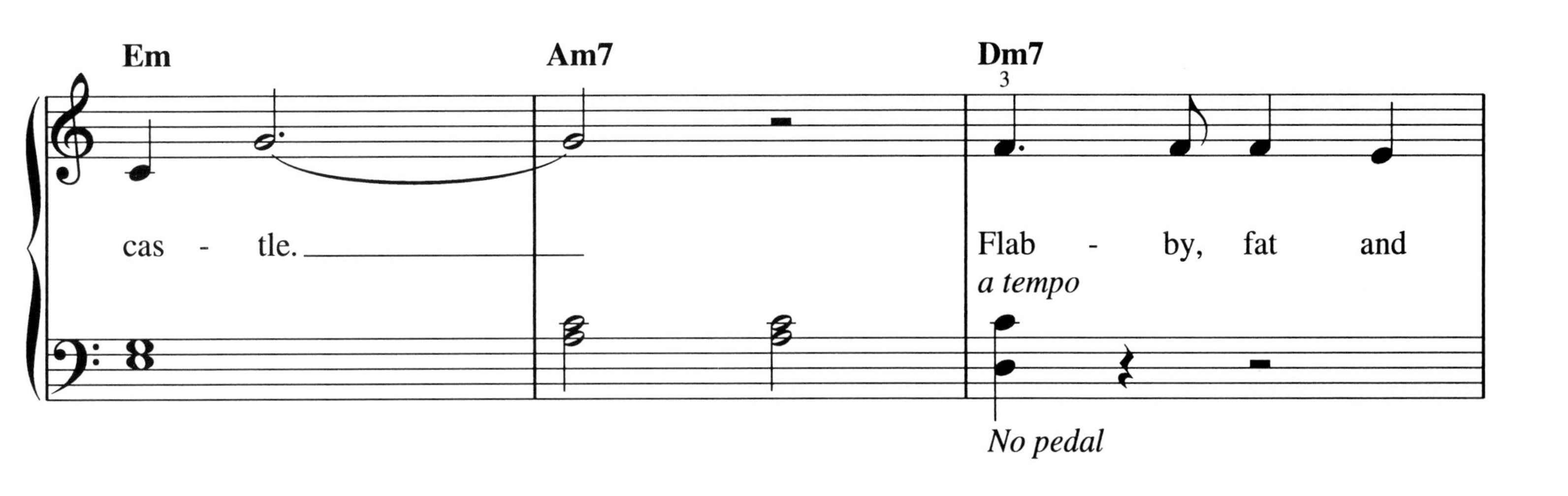
Em
Am7
Dm7
3
cas - tle. Flab - by, fat and
a tempo
No pedal

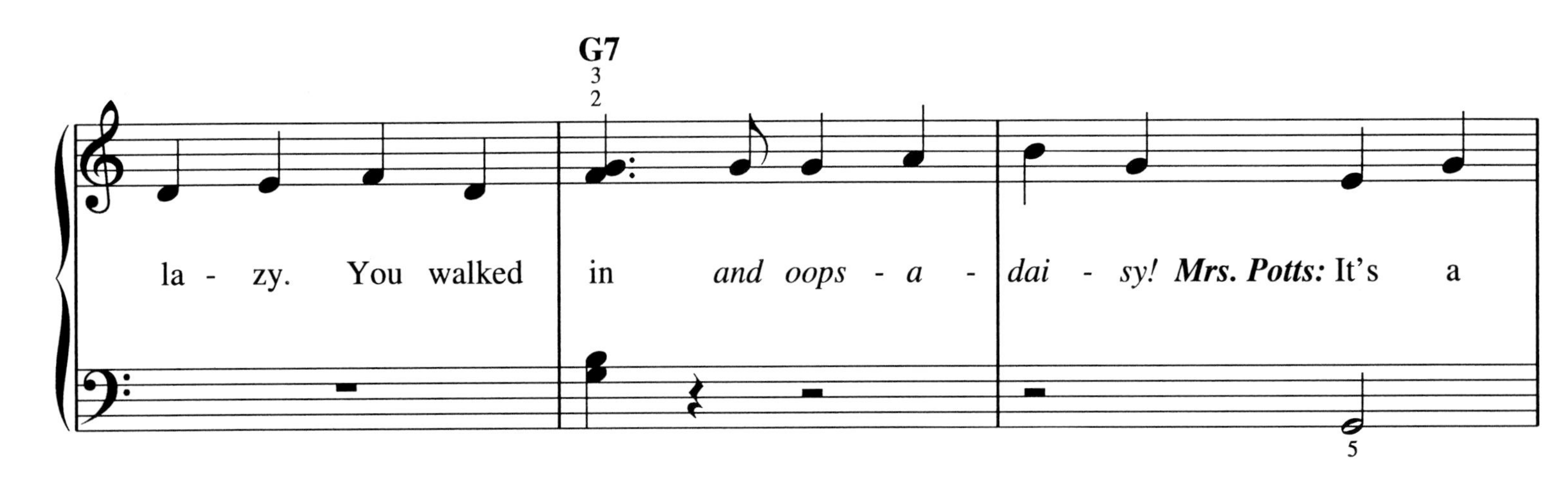
G7
la - zy. You walked in and oops - a - dai - sy! Mrs. Potts: It's a

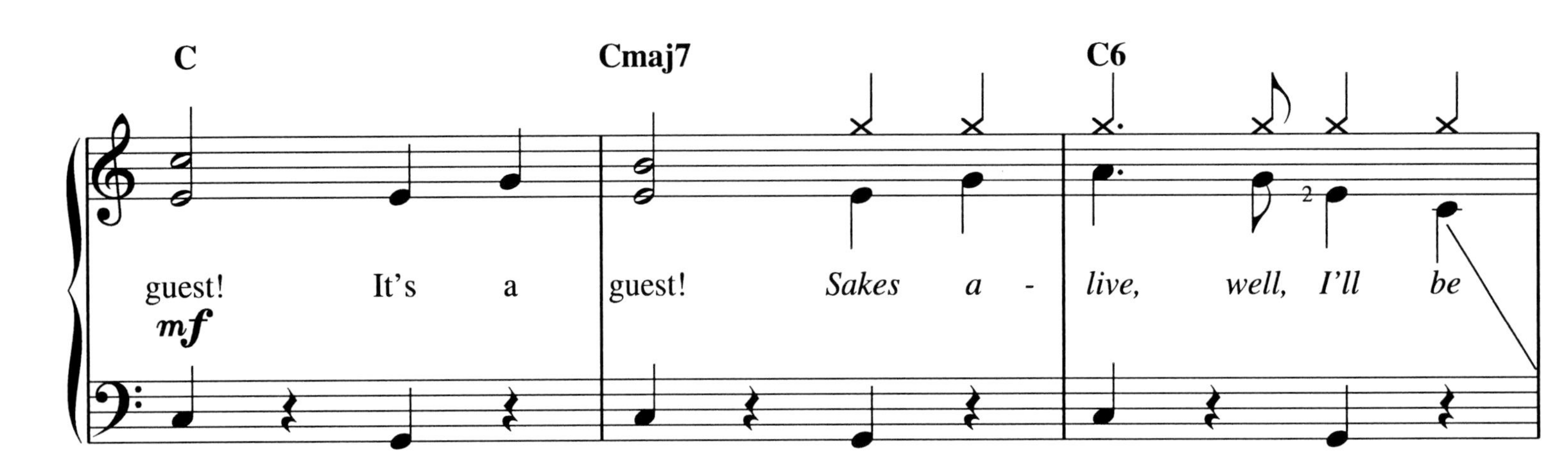
C
Cmaj7
C6
guest! It's a guest! Sakes a - live, well, I'll be
mf

C
C♯dim
blessed! Wine's been poured and thank the Lord I've had the

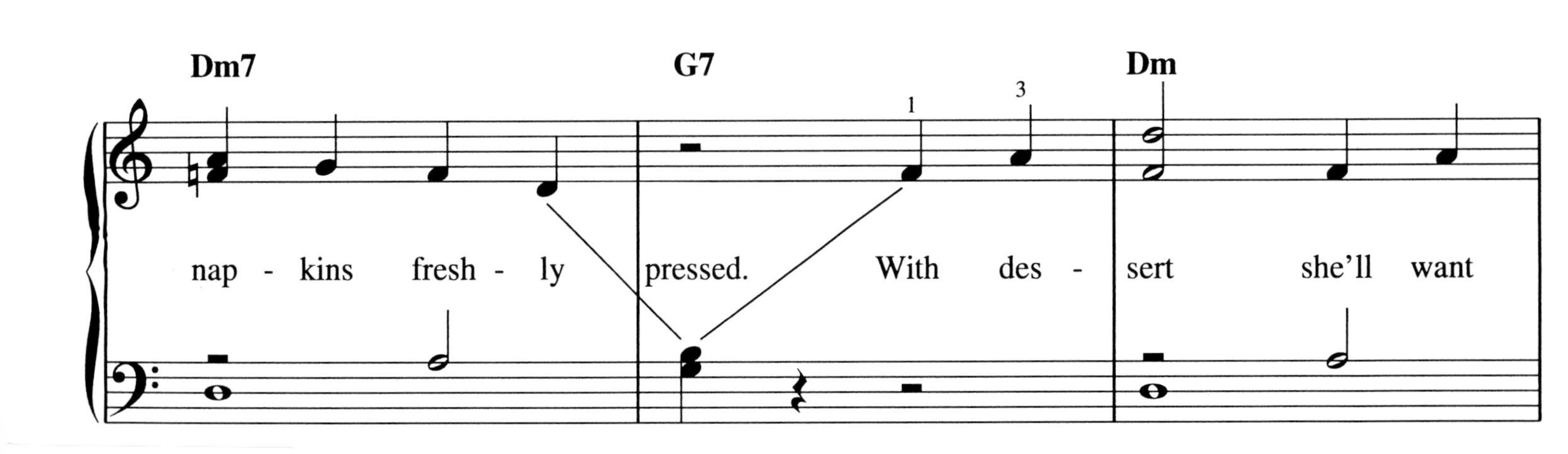
Dm7
G7
Dm
nap - kins fresh - ly pressed. With des - sert she'll want

Dm♯7
Dm7
G
tea. And my
dear, that's fine with
me. While the

Dm7
D♯dim
Em
E♭dim
cups do their soft
shoe - ing, I'll be
bub - bling! I'll be

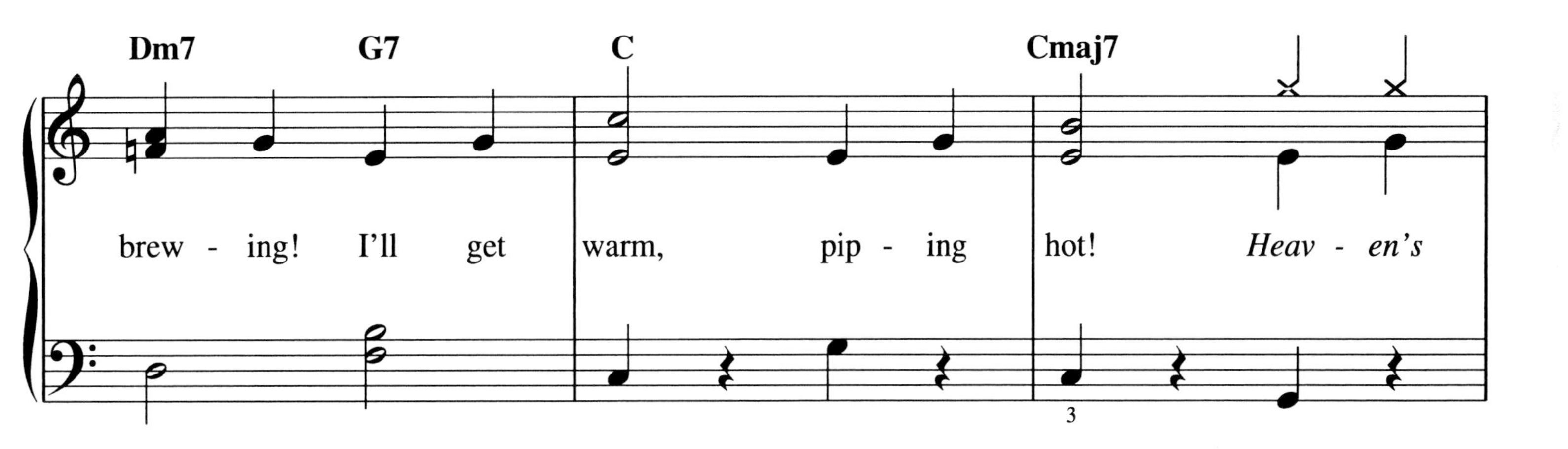
Dm7
G7
C
Cmaj7
brew - ing! I'll get
warm, pip - ing
hot! Heav - en's

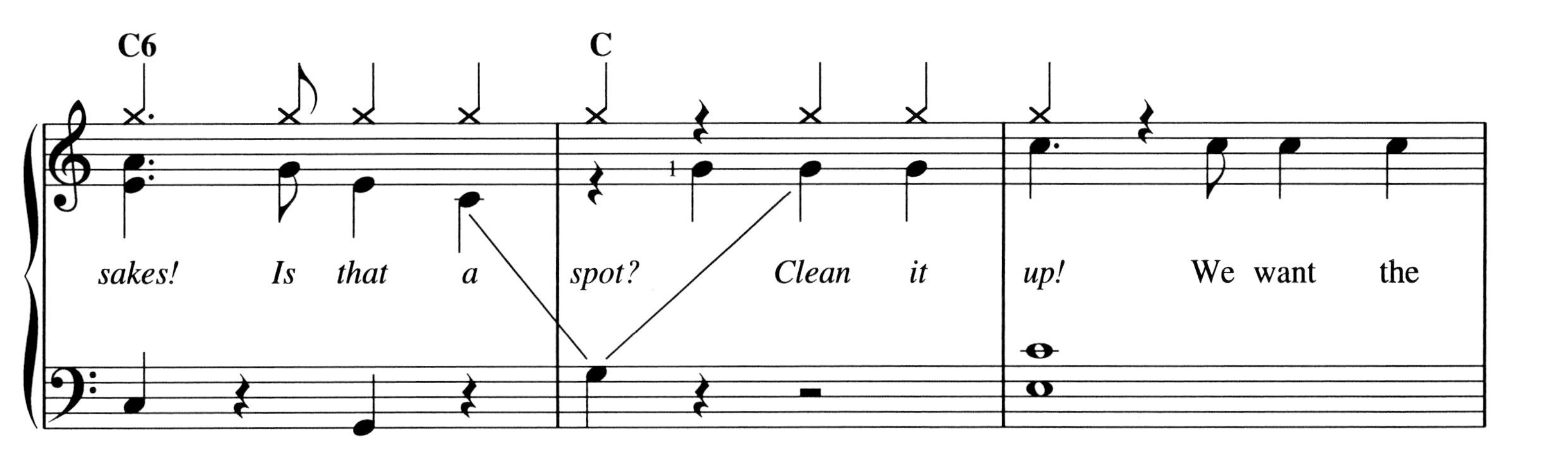
C6
C
sakes! Is that a
spot? Clean it
up! We want the

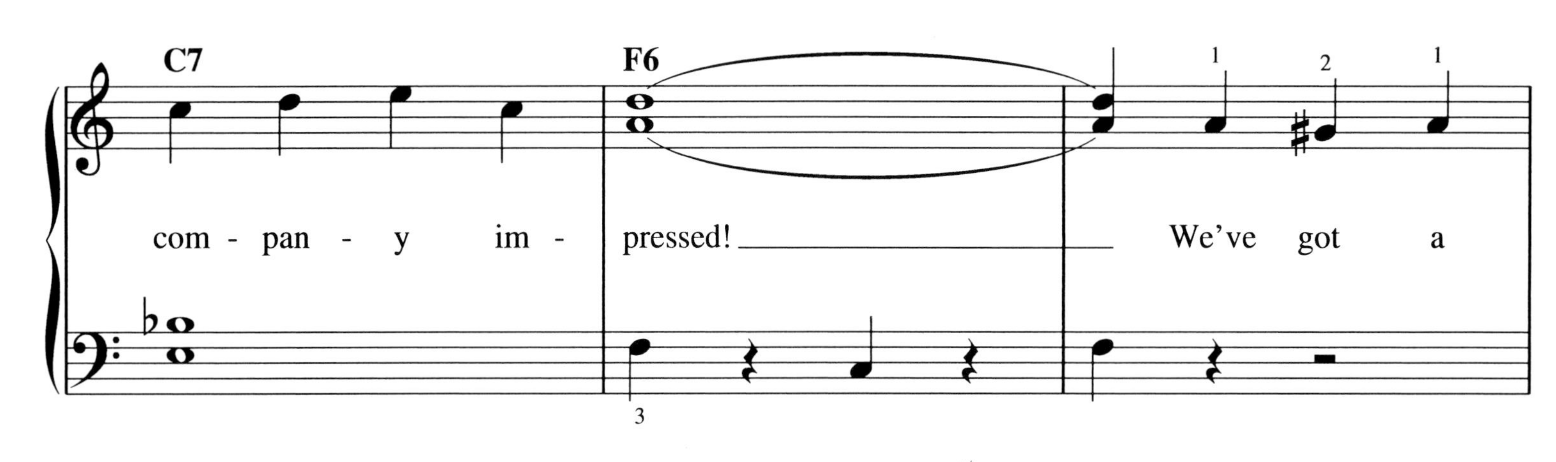
C7
F6
com - pan - y im - pressed! We've got a

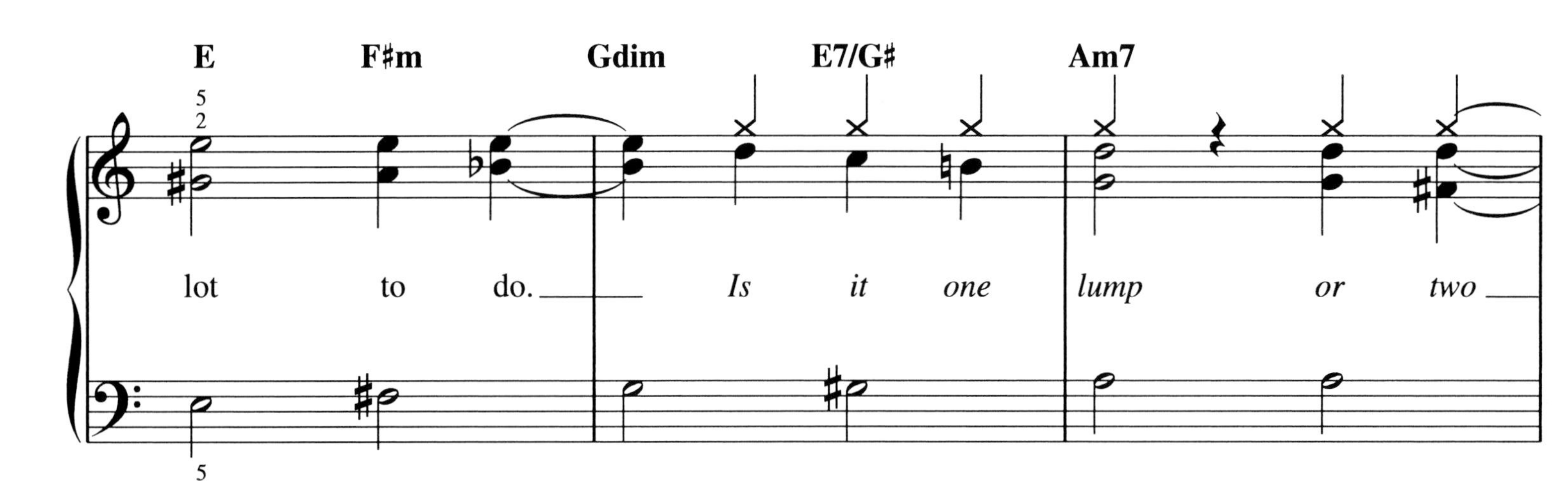
E
F#m
Gdim
E7/G#
Am7
lot to do. Is it one lump or two

D7
Dm7
G7
for you, our guest? Chorus: She's our guest! Mrs. Potts: She's our

Em
D7
G
guest! Chorus: She's our guest! Be our guest! Be our

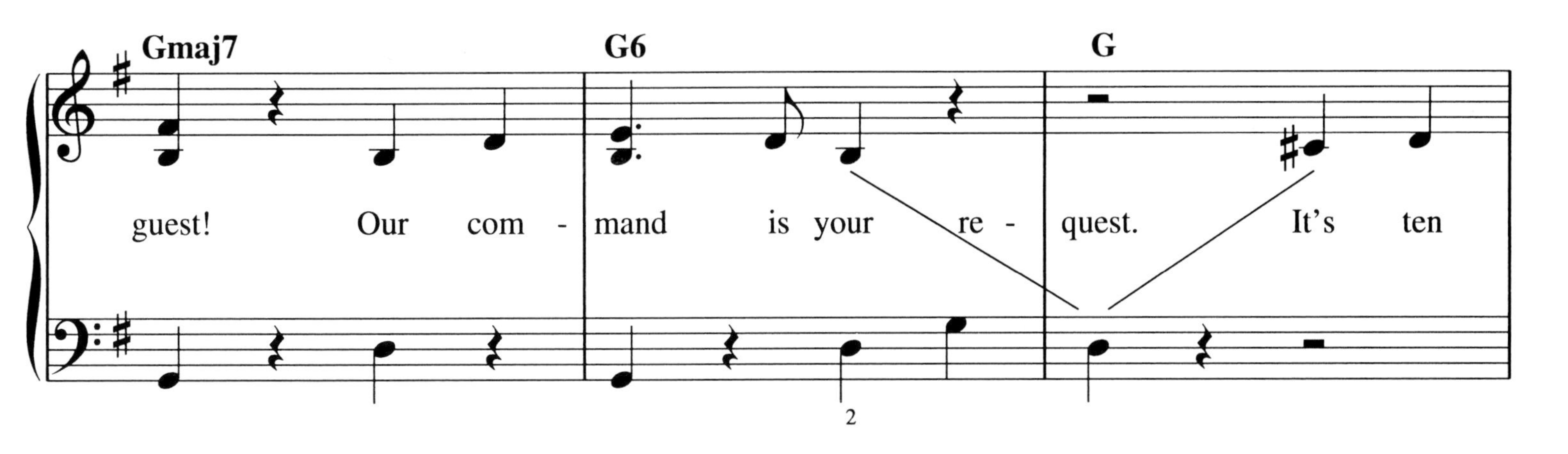
Gmaj7
G6
G
guest! Our com - mand is your re - quest. It's ten
2

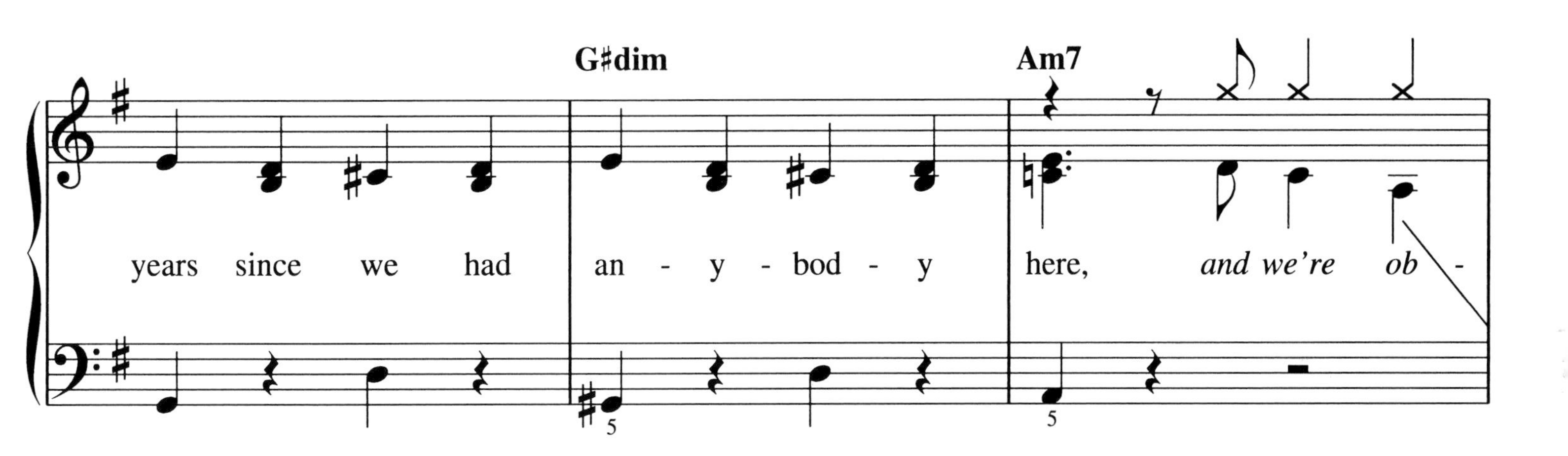
G♯dim
Am7
years since we had an - y - bod - y here, and we're ob -
5
5

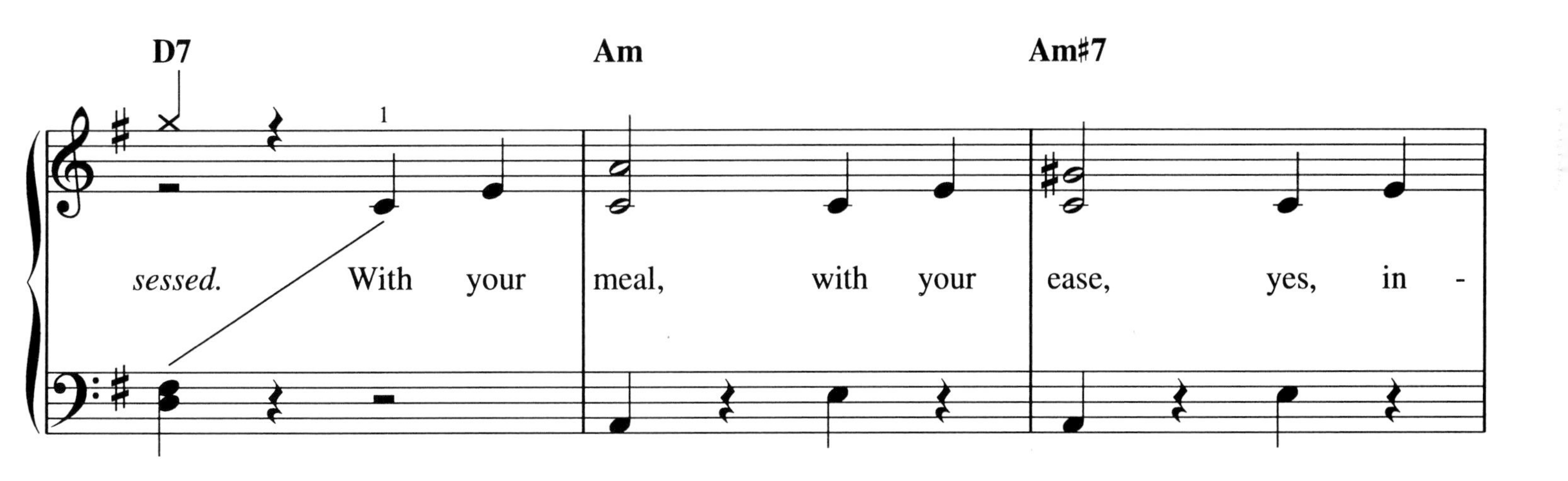
D7
Am
Am♯7
1
sessed. With your meal, with your ease, yes, in -

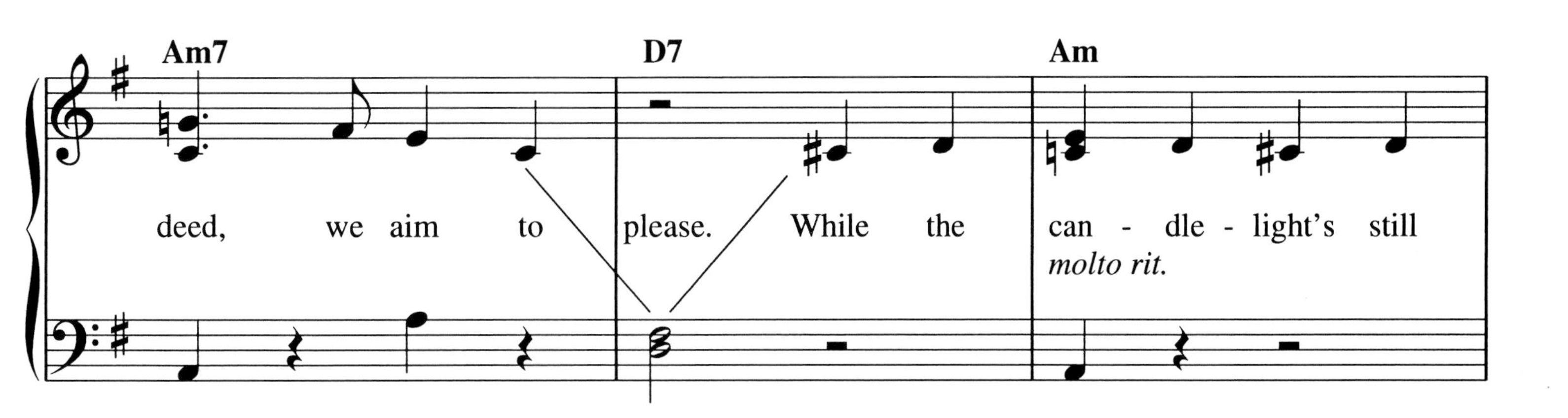
Am7
D7
Am
deed, we aim to please. While the can - dle - light's still
molto rit.

D7
G7
glow - ing let us
help you, we'll keep
rit.
go - ing course by

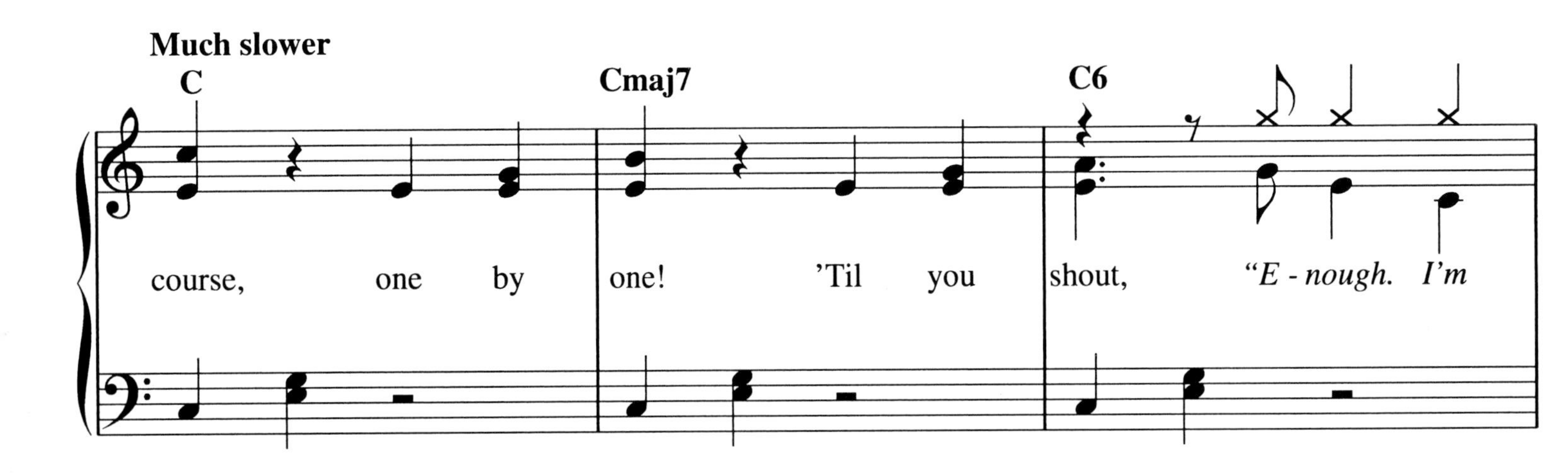
Much slower
C
Cmaj7
C6
course, one by
one! 'Til you
shout, "E - nough. I'm

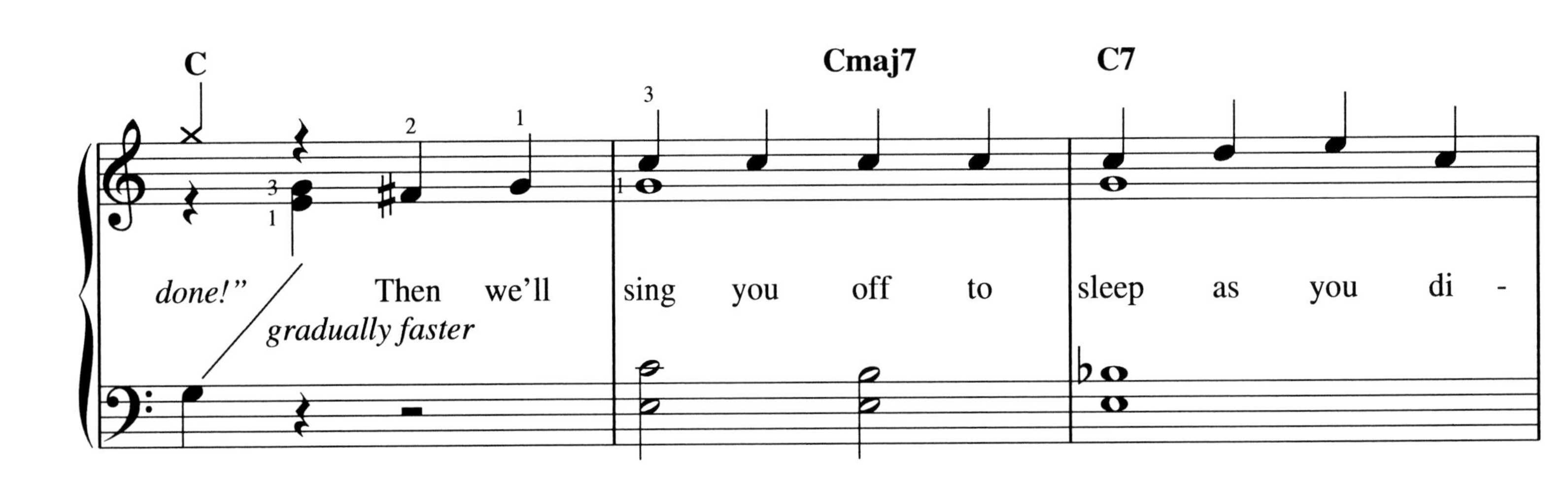
C
Cmaj7
C7
done!" Then we'll
gradually faster
sing you off to
sleep as you di -

F6
E
F♯m7
gest.
To - night you'll
prop your feet
a tempo

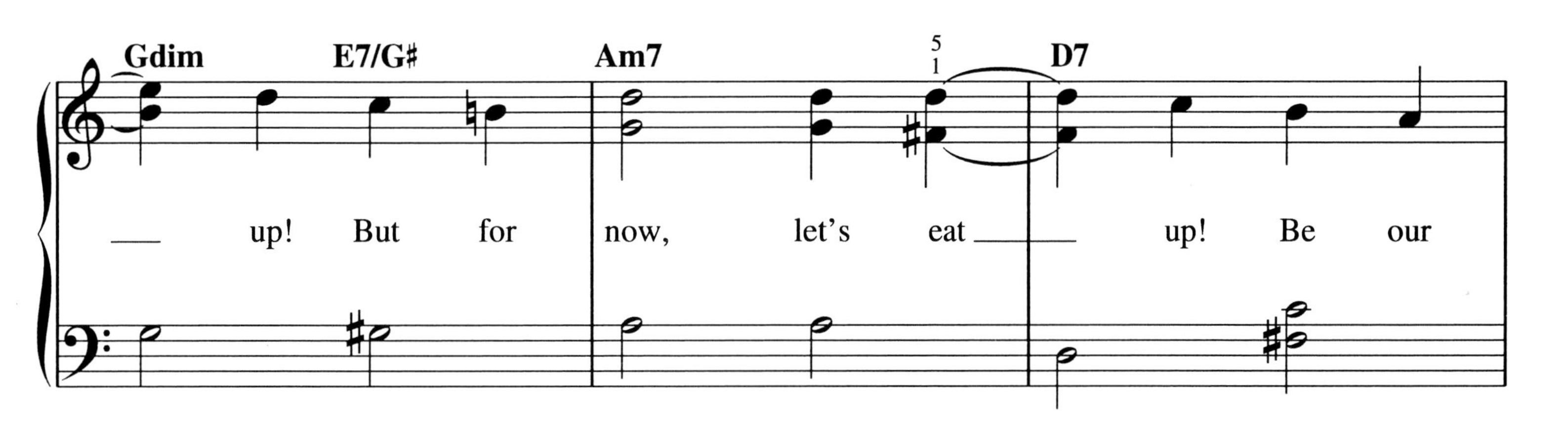
Gdim
E7/G♯
Am7
D7
up! But for now, let's eat up! Be our

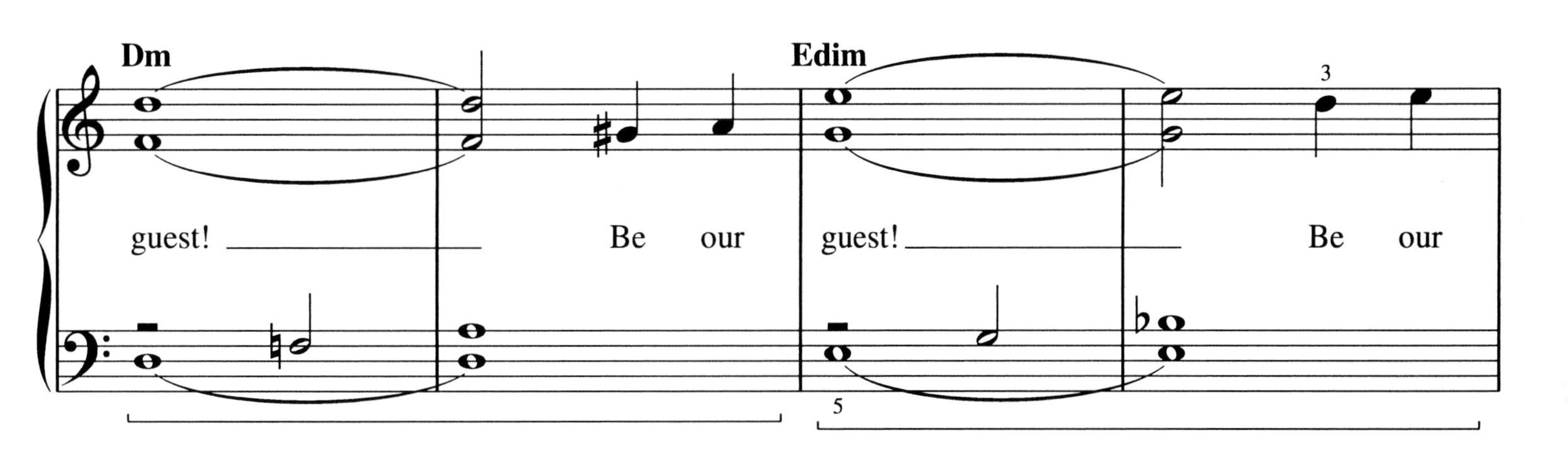
Dm
Edim
guest! Be our guest! Be our

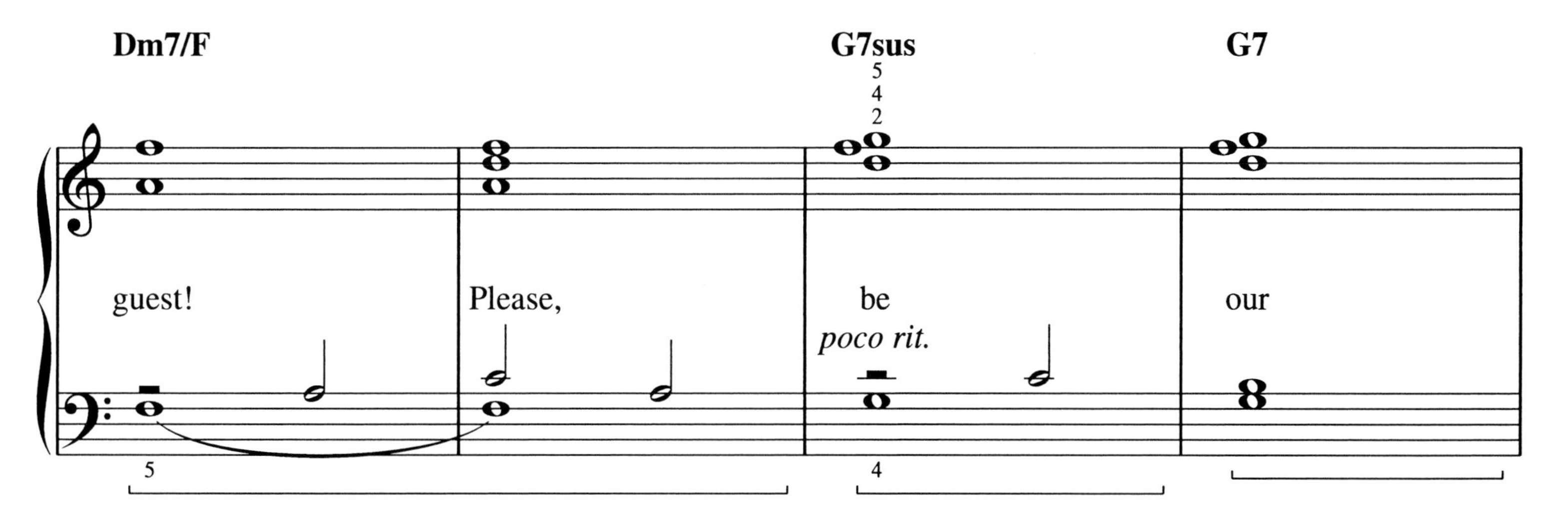
Dm7/F
G7sus
G7
guest! Please, be our
poco rit.

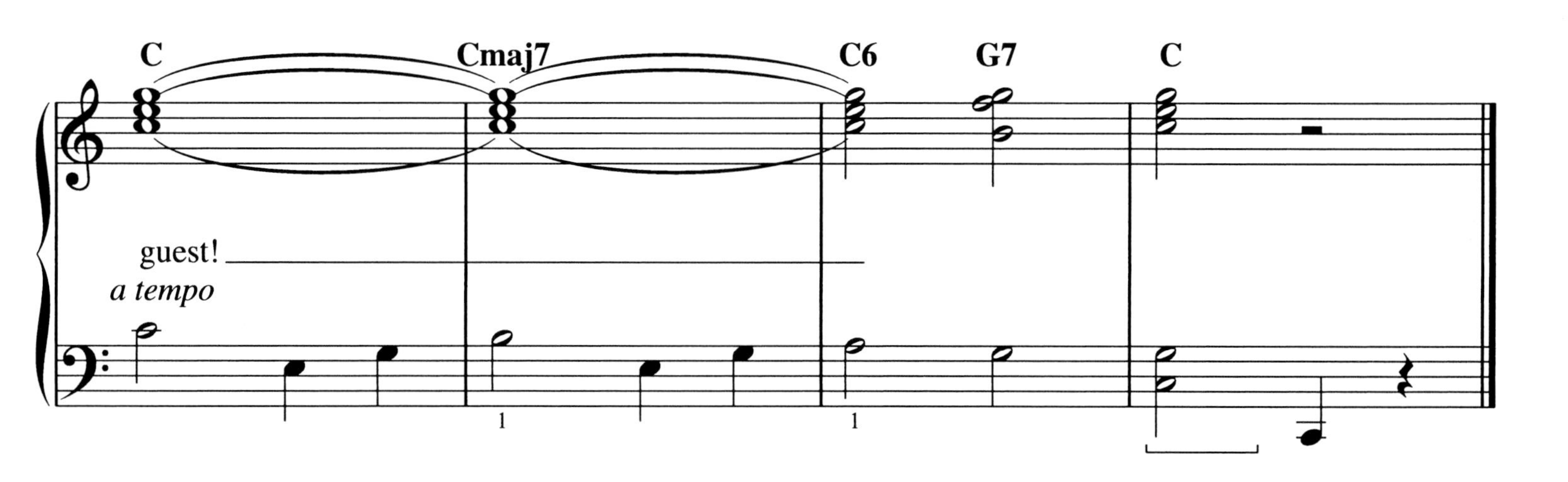
C
Cmaj7
C6
G7
C
guest!
a tempo

SOMETHING THERE

Lyrics by HOWARD ASHMAN
Music by ALAN MENKEN

G7sus
G7
C
G7sus
G7
E♭
B♭7sus
B♭7
G7sus
No pedal
G7
Beast: She glanced this
2.
C
fore.
F
C/E
Dm7
Dm7/G
Emadd9
Belle: New,
and a bit a - larm - ing.

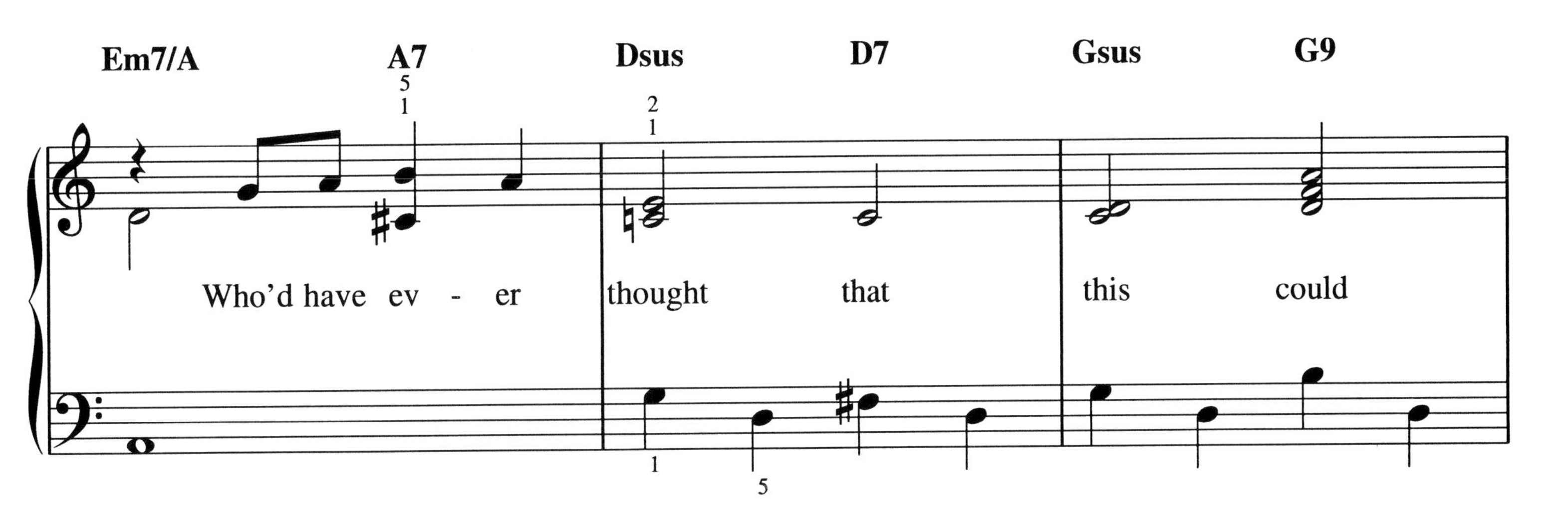
Em7/A
A7
Dsus
D7
Gsus
G9
Who'd have ev - er thought that this could

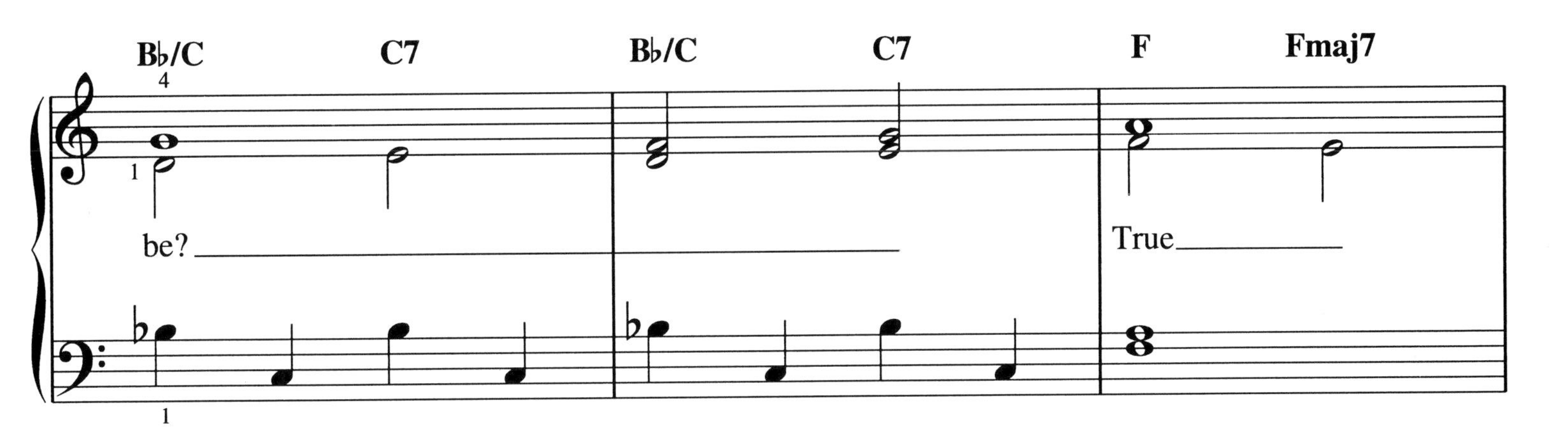
B♭/C
C7
B♭/C
C7
F
Fmaj7
be?
True

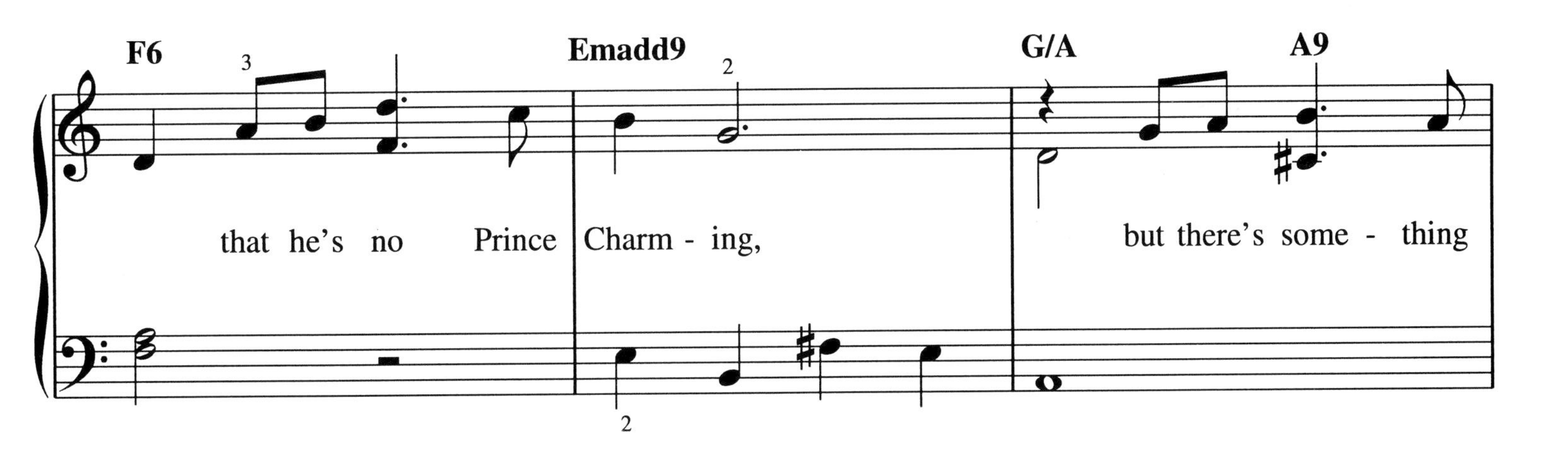
F6
Emadd9
G/A
A9
that he's no Prince Charm - ing, but there's some - thing

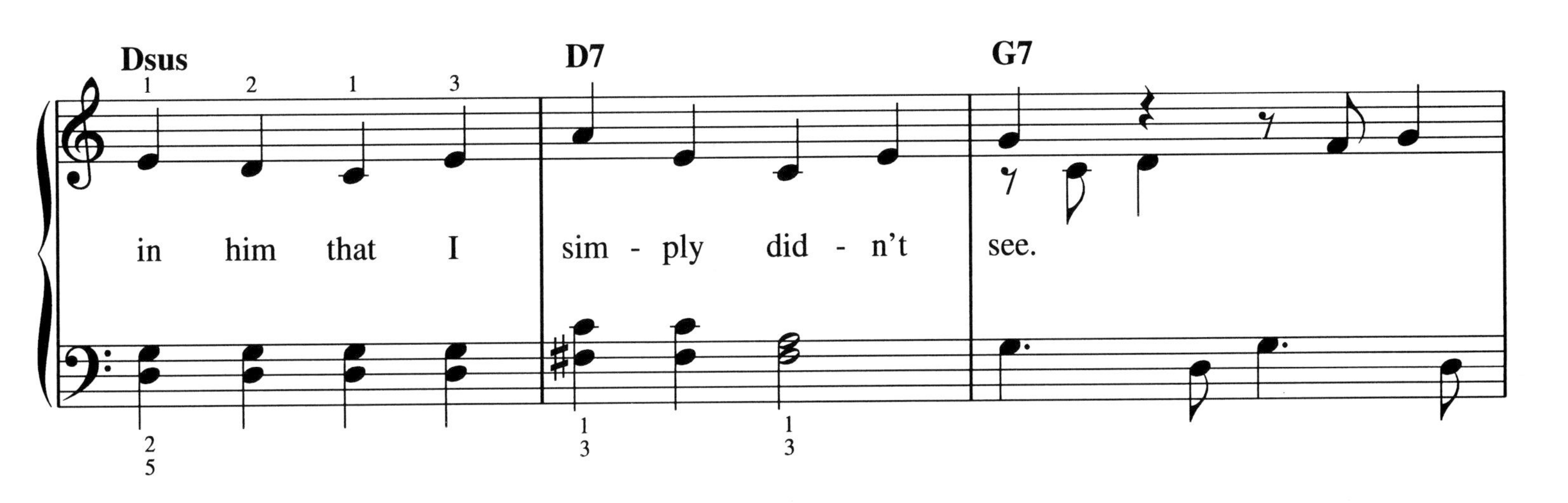
Dsus
D7
G7
in him that I sim - ply did - n't see.

G7sus/C
G7/B
Mrs. Potts: Well, bless my soul.
Lumiere: Well, who'd have thought?
Cogsworth: Well, who'd have

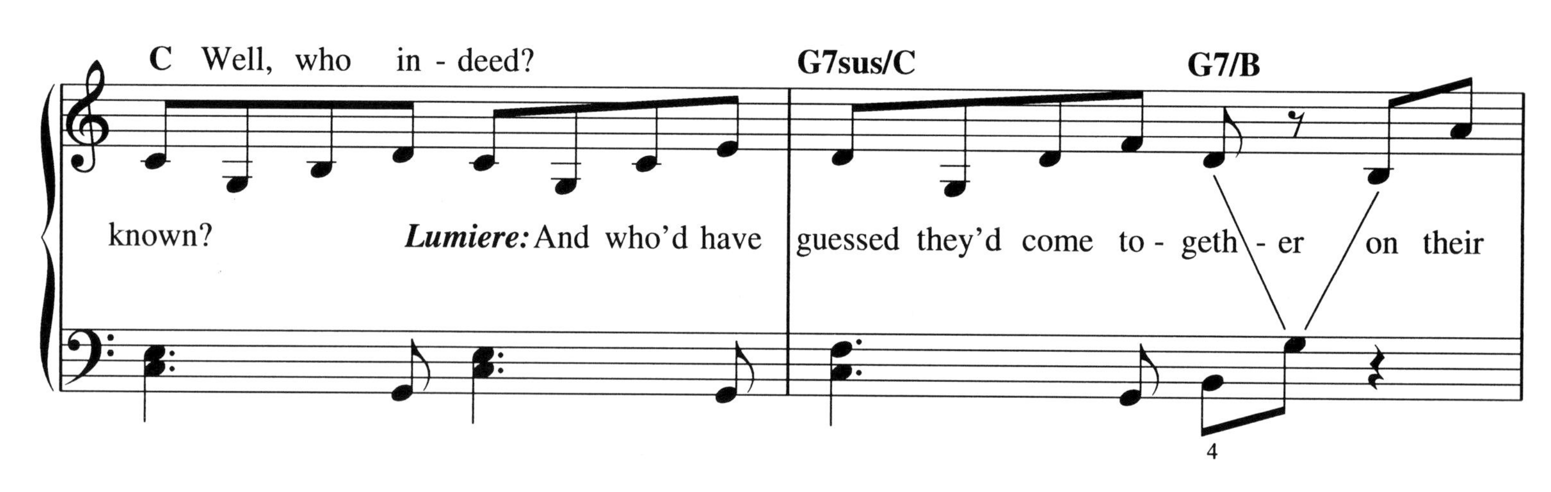
C
Well, who in - deed?
G7sus/C
G7/B
known?
Lumiere: And who'd have
guessed they'd come to - geth - er on their

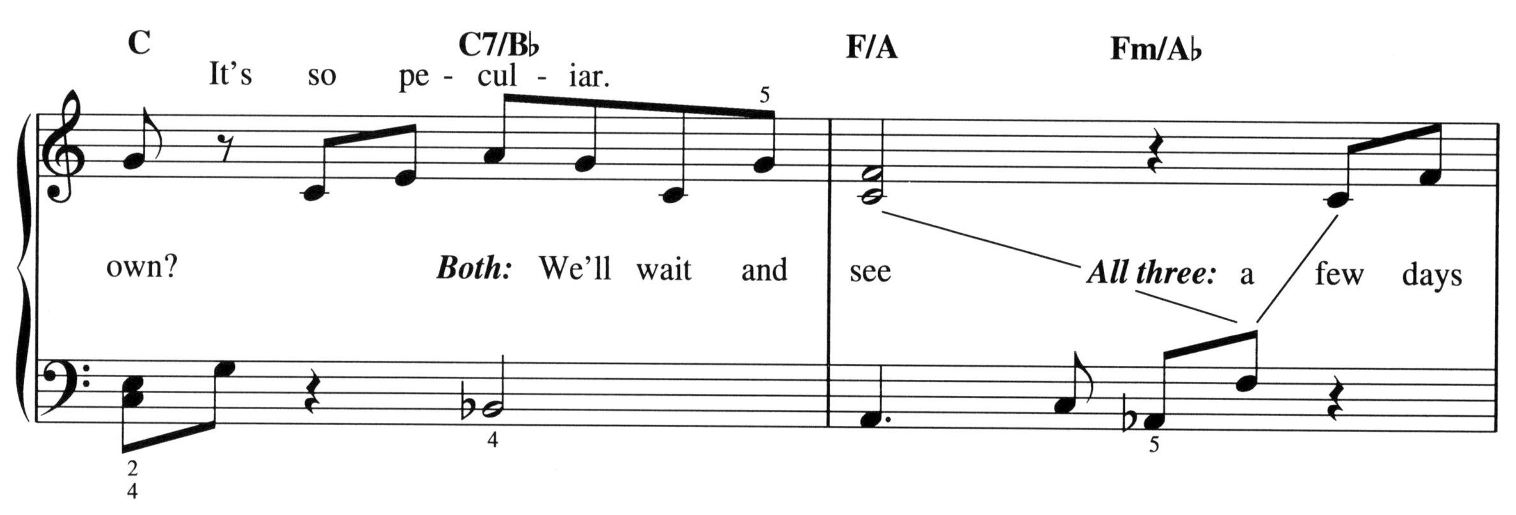
C
C7/B♭
It's so pe - cul - iar.
F/A
Fm/A♭
own?
Both: We'll wait and
see
All three: a few days

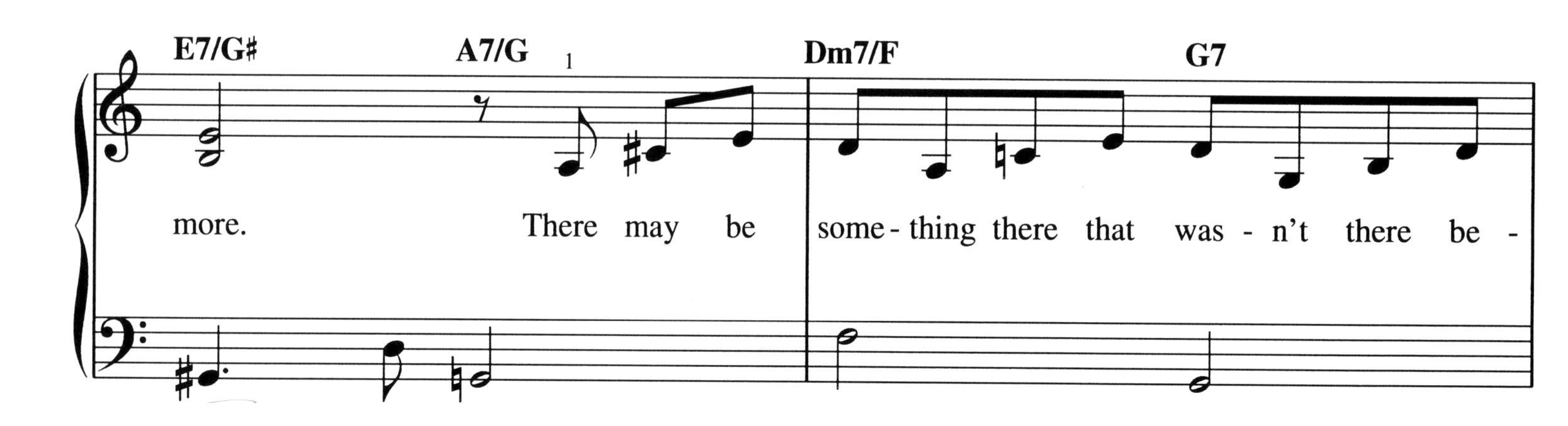
E7/G#
A7/G
Dm7/F
G7
more.
There may be
some - thing there that was - n't there be -

Cadd9
C
G7sus
G7/B
fore. Cogsworth: You know, perhaps there's something there that was-n't there be-

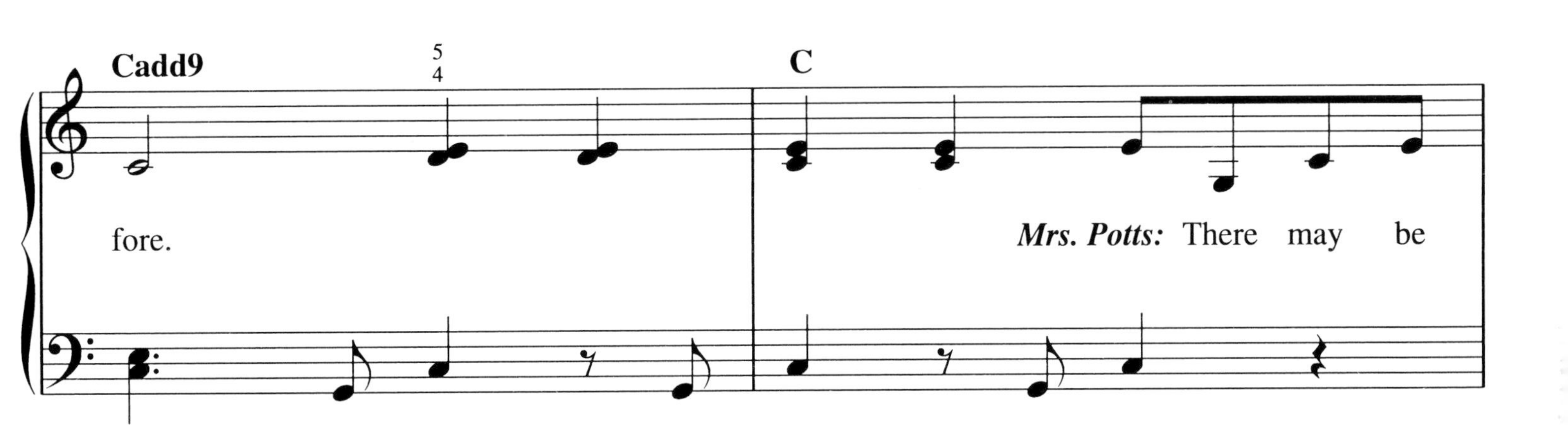
Cadd9
C
fore.
Mrs. Potts: There may be

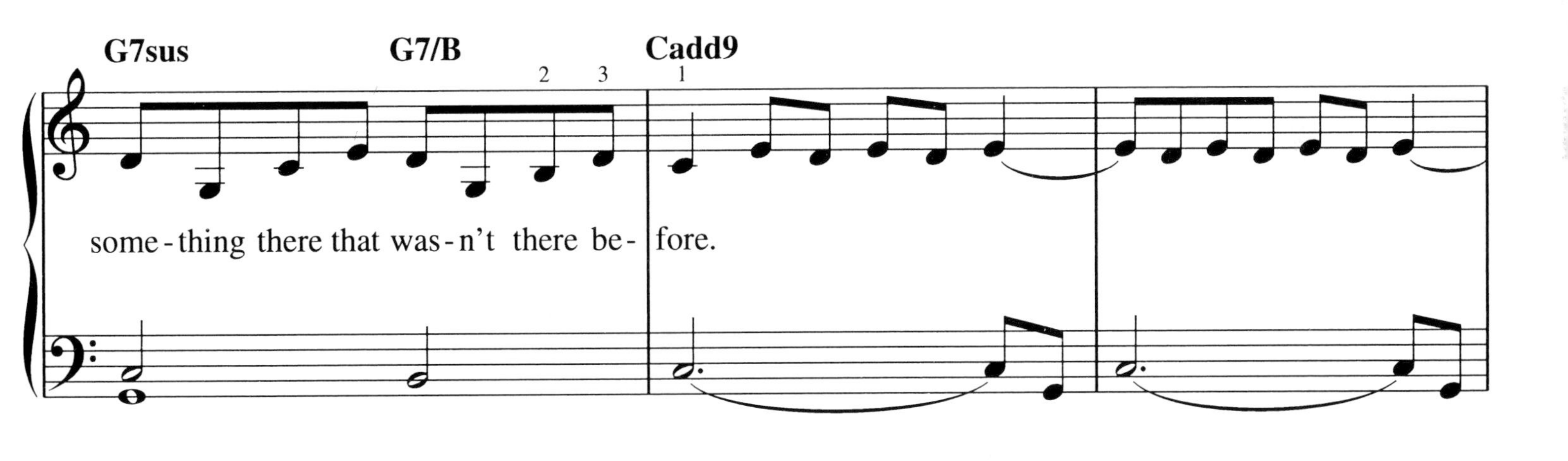
G7sus
G7/B
Cadd9
some-thing there that was-n't there be-
fore.

rit.

THE MOB SONG

Lyrics by HOWARD ASHMAN
Music by ALAN MENKEN

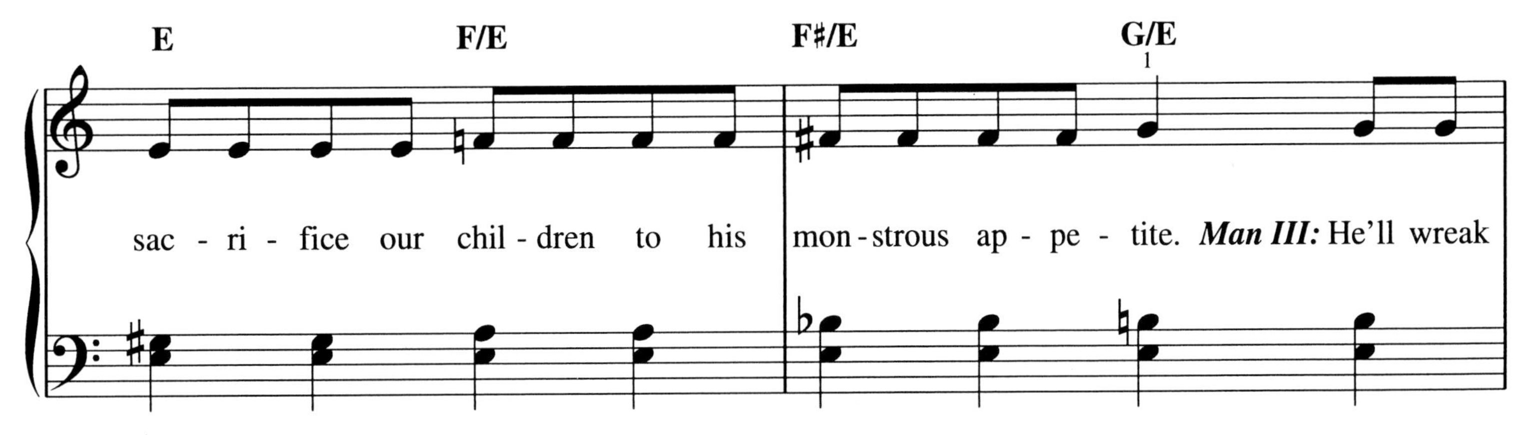

E
Am/E
E7
Am/E
ha - voc on our vil - lage if we
let him wan - der free. *Gaston:* So it's

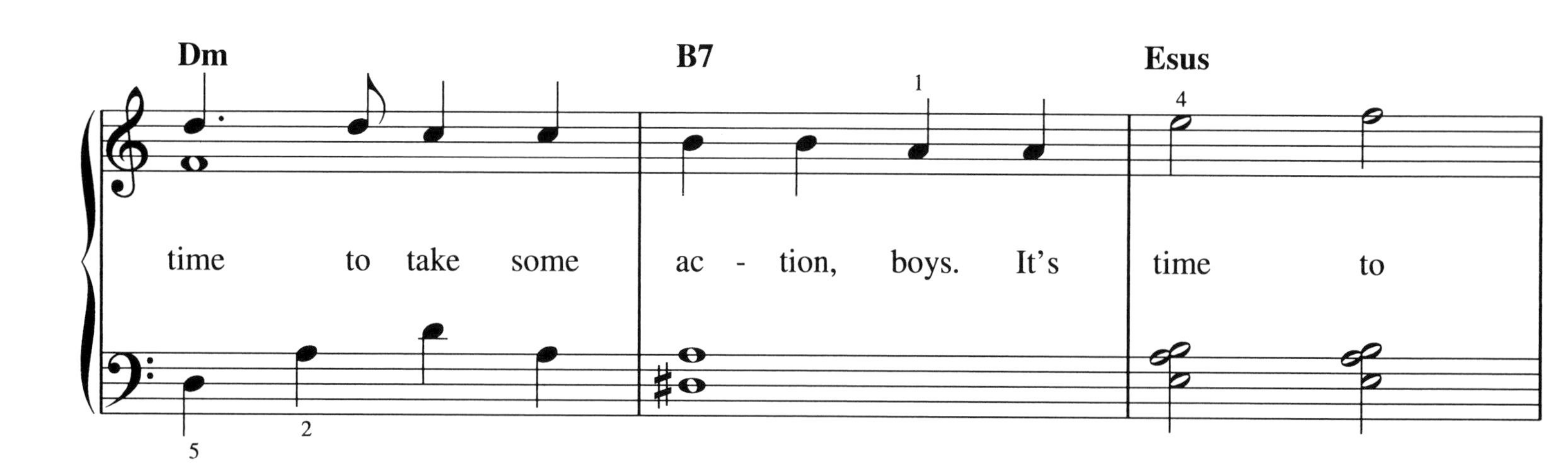
Dm
B7
Esus
time to take some
ac - tion, boys. It's
time to

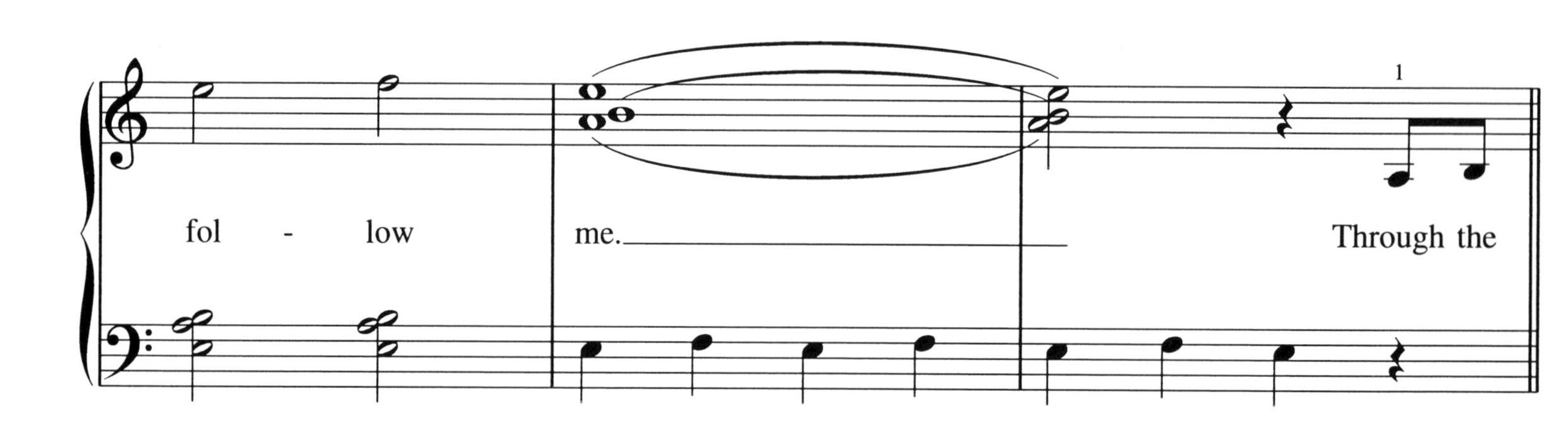
fol - low
me.
Through the

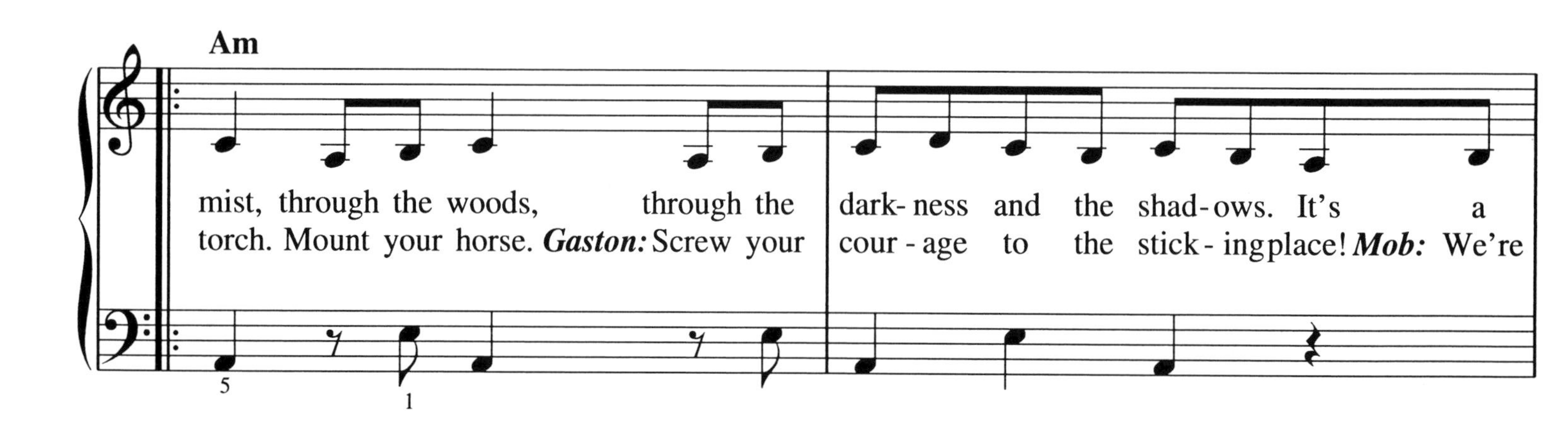
Am
mist, through the woods, through the
dark- ness and the shad- ows. It's a
torch. Mount your horse. *Gaston:* Screw your
cour - age to the stick - ing place! *Mob:* We're

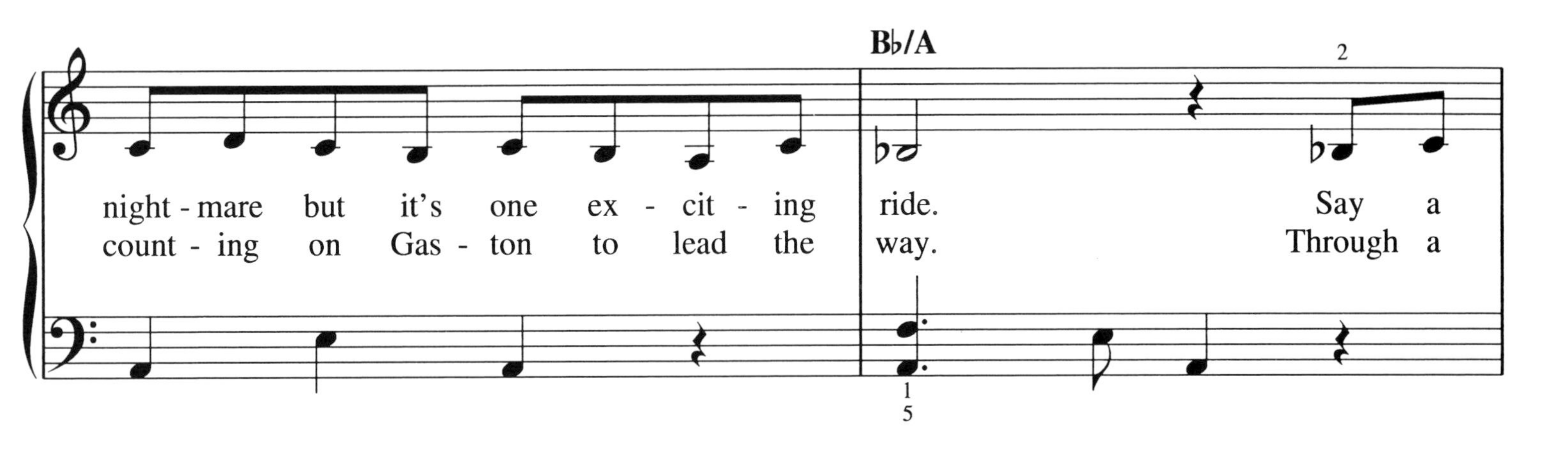
B♭/A
night-mare but it's one ex-cit-ing ride. Say a
count-ing on Gas-ton to lead the way. Through a

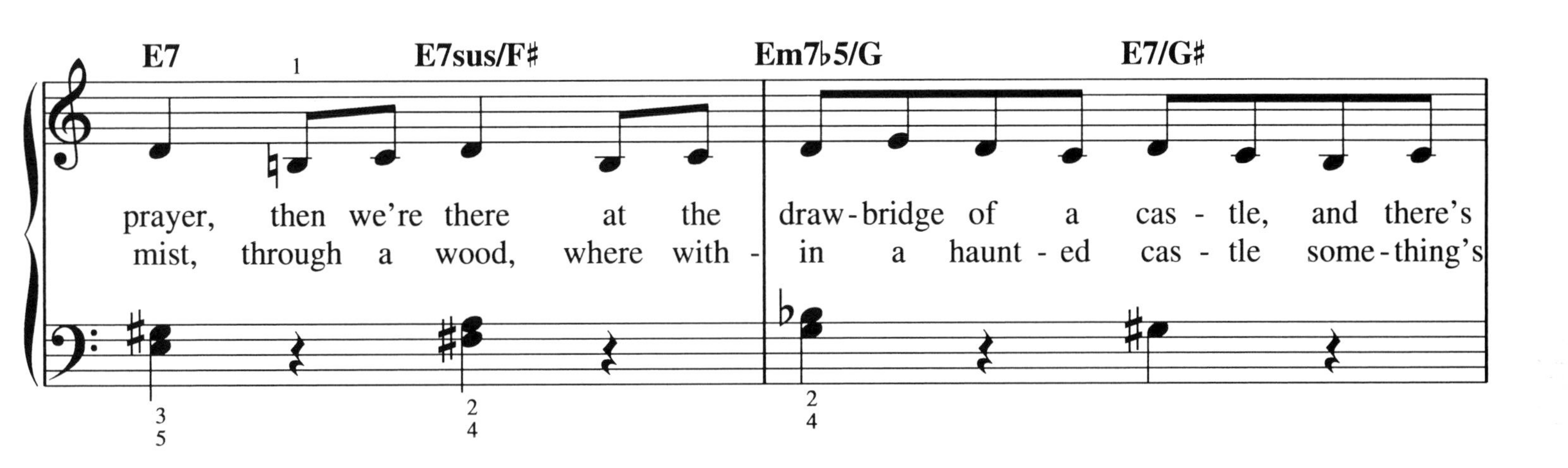
E7 E7sus/F♯ Em7♭5/G E7/G♯
prayer, then we're there at the draw-bridge of a cas-tle, and there's
mist, through a wood, where with-in a haunt-ed cas-tle some-thing's

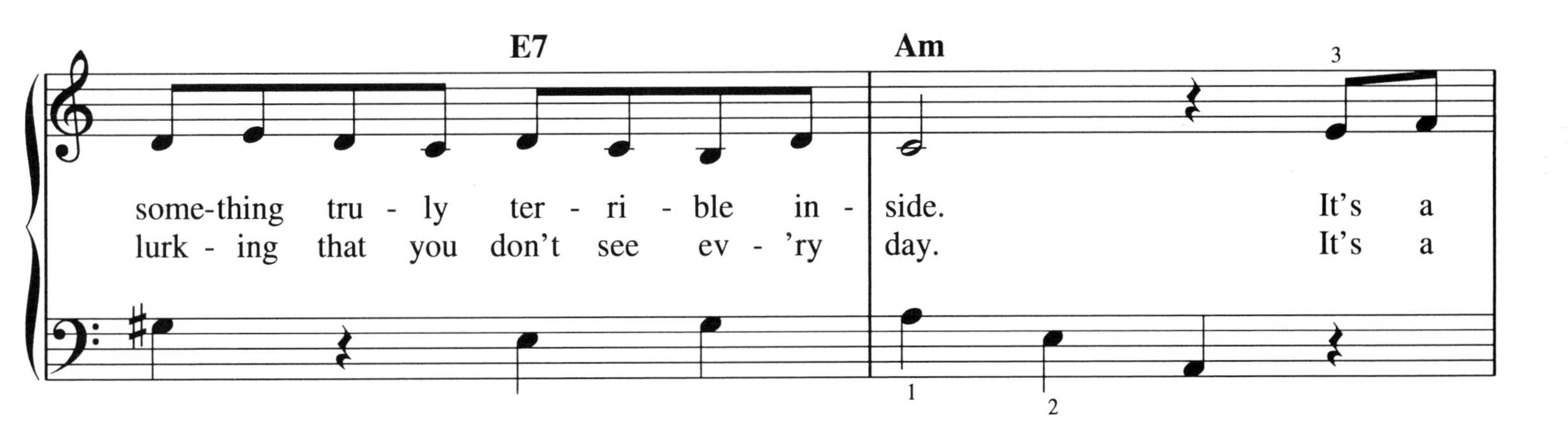
E7 Am
some-thing tru-ly ter-ri-ble in-side. It's a
lurk-ing that you don't see ev-'ry day. It's a

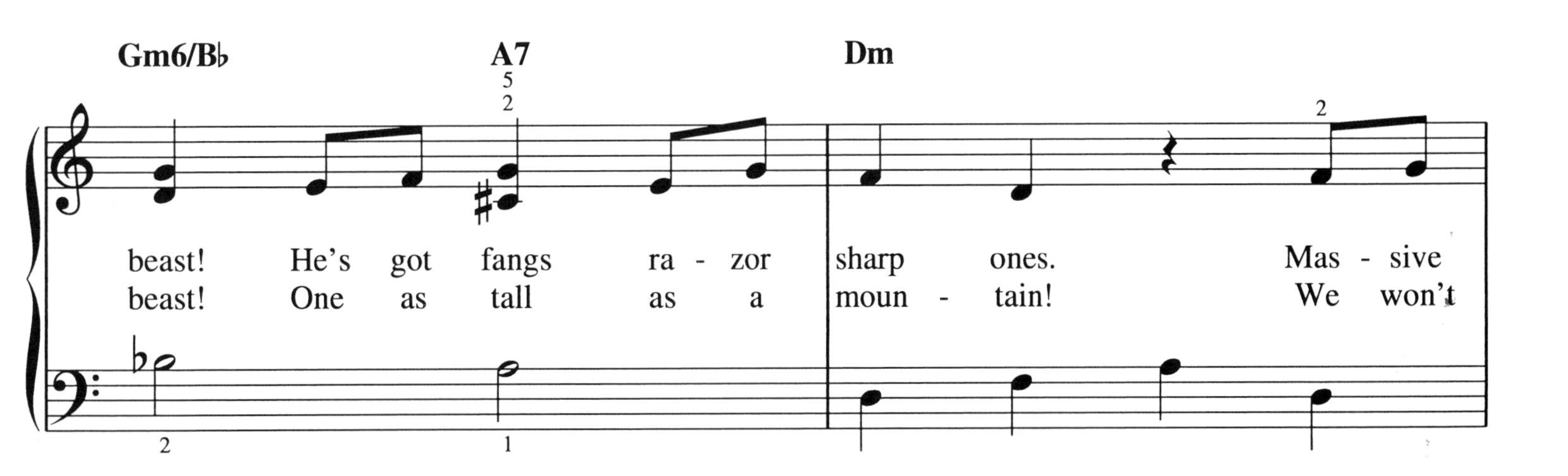
Gm6/B♭ A7 Dm
beast! He's got fangs ra-zor sharp ones. Mas-sive
beast! One as tall as a moun-tain! We won't

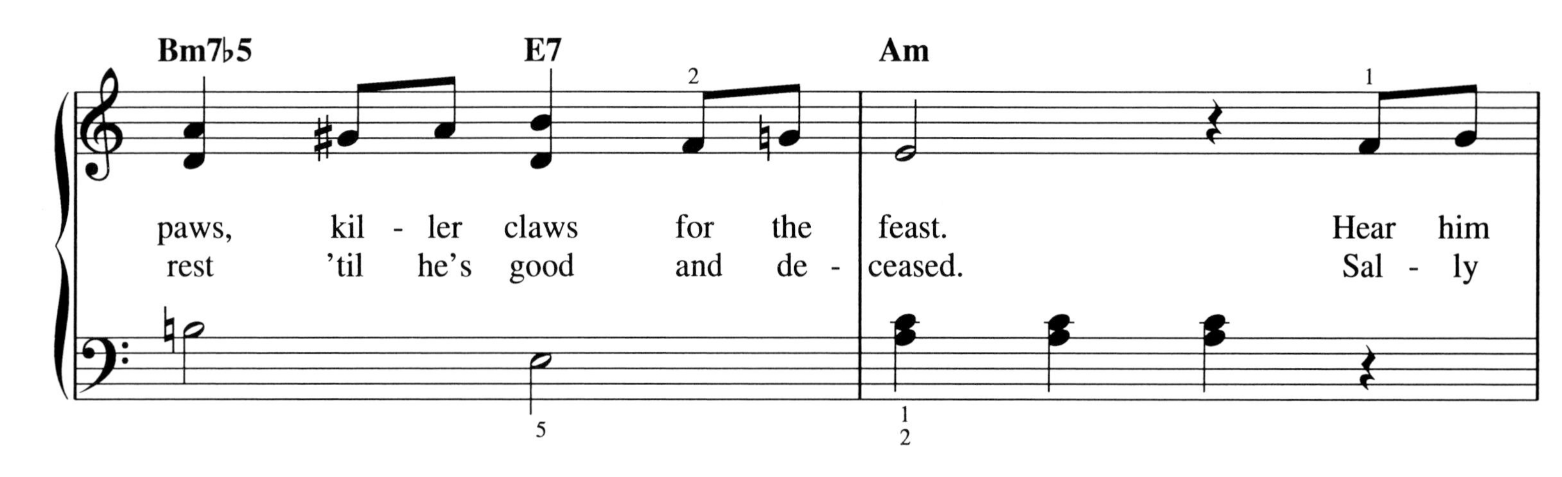
Bm7♭5
E7
Am
paws, kil - ler claws for the feast. Hear him
rest 'til he's good and de - ceased. Sal - ly

F
G/F
C/E
(1) 2nd time Dm
roar! See him foam! But we're not com - ing home 'til he's
forth! Tal - ly ho! Grab your sword! Grab your bow! Praise the

1.
Bm7♭5
Esus
E
Am
dead! Good and dead! Kill the Beast! Belle: No! I won't let you
mp
Add pedal

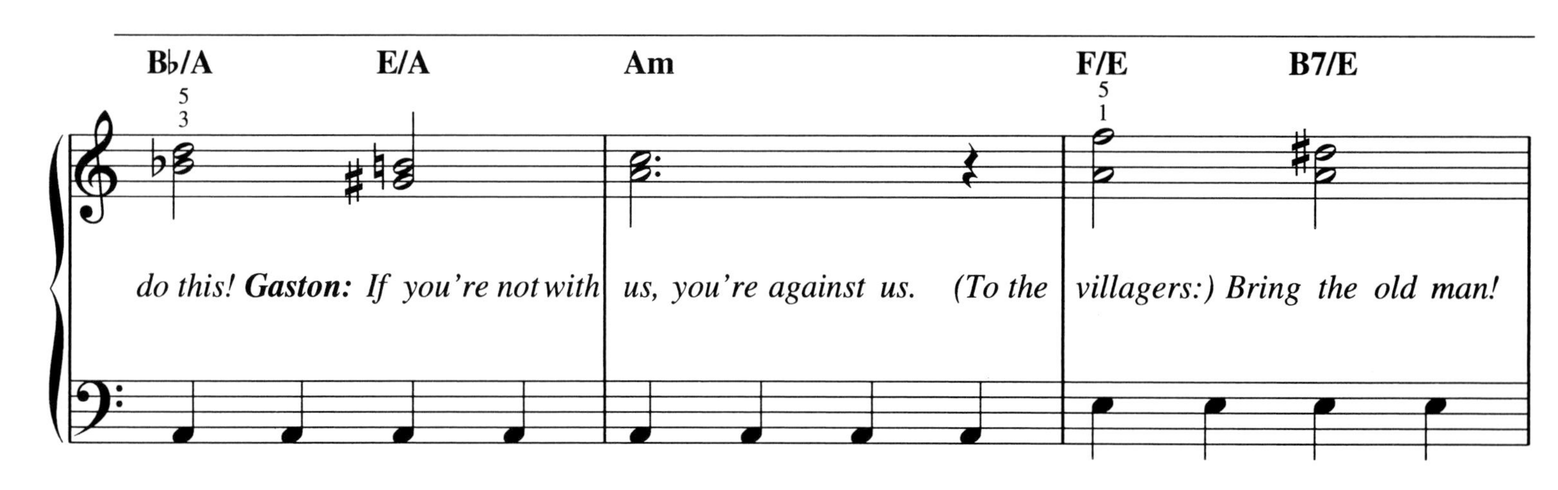
B♭/A
E/A
Am
F/E
B7/E
do this! Gaston: If you're not with us, you're against us. (To the villagers:) Bring the old man!

E
Em7♭5
A
Dm
Maurice: Get your hands off me! Gaston: We can't have them running off to warn the creature! Belle: Let us
Bm7♭5
B7
Esus
out! Gaston: We'll rid the village of this Beast! Who's with me? Mob: I am! I am!
cresc.
Stop pedal
E
I am! Light your
f
2.
Bm7♭5
Lord and here we go! Gaston: We'll lay
Esus
siege to the castle and bring back his head!
mp

F
D/F♯
G
Dm/F
E
Belle: I have to warn the Beast! This is all my fault! Oh, Papa, what are

Am
G/B
C7/B♭
F/A
we going to do? Maurice: Now, now, we'll think of something.

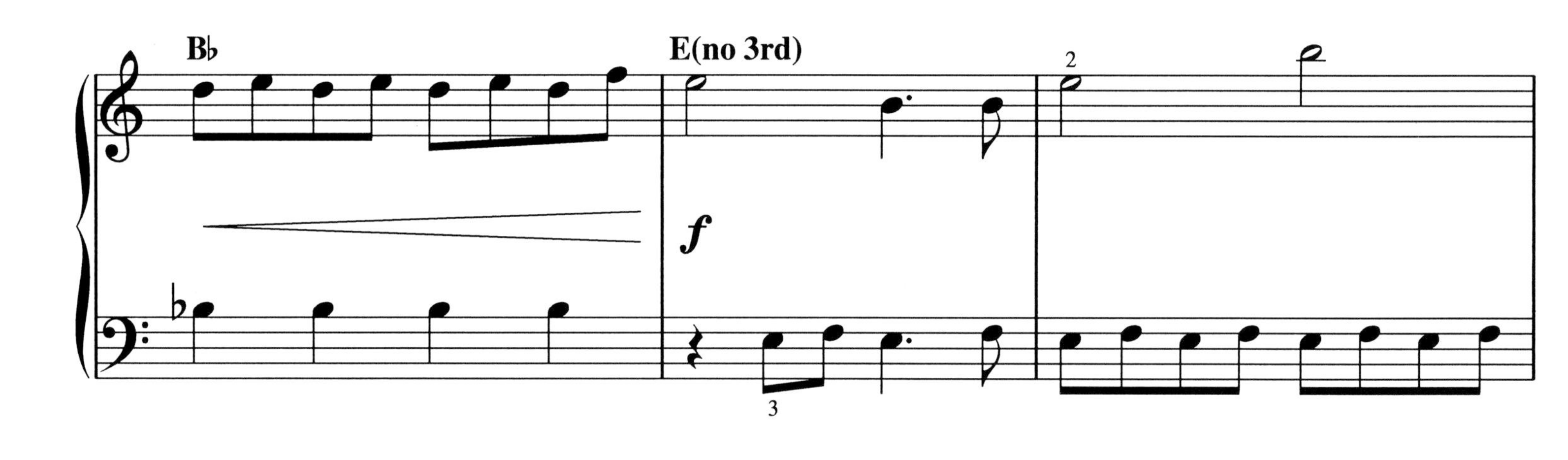
B♭
E(no 3rd)

Am
Mob: We don't like what we don't un - der - stand in fact, it scares us and this

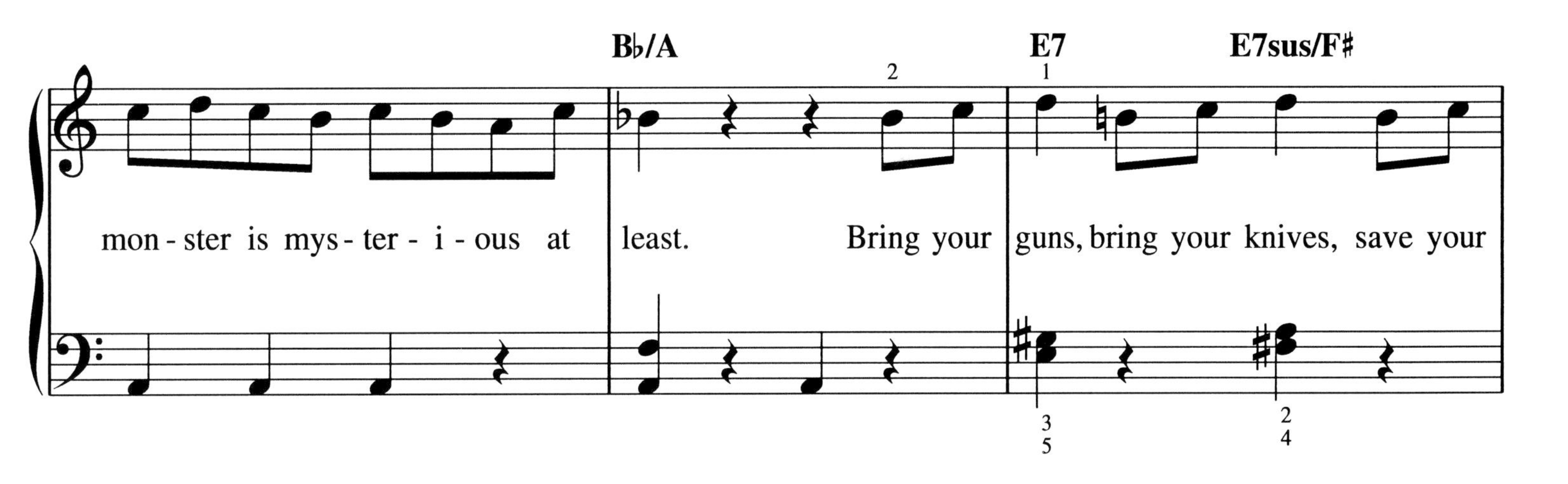
B♭/A
E7
E7sus/F♯
mon - ster is mys - ter - i - ous at
least. Bring your
guns, bring your knives, save your

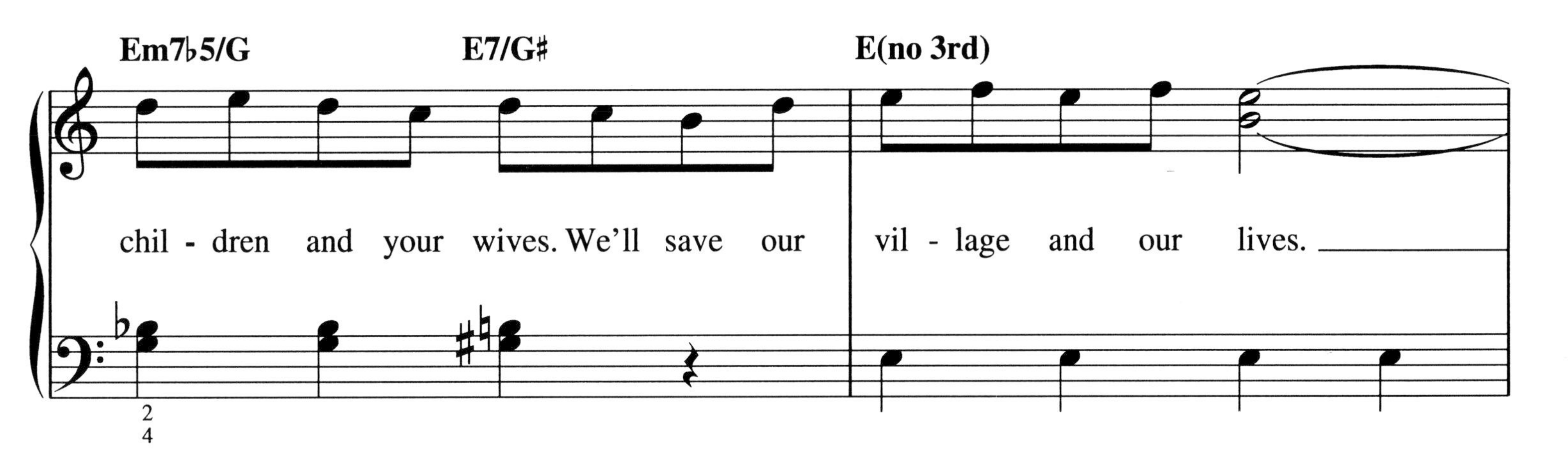
Em7♭5/G
E7/G♯
E(no 3rd)
chil - dren and your wives. We'll save our
vil - lage and our lives.

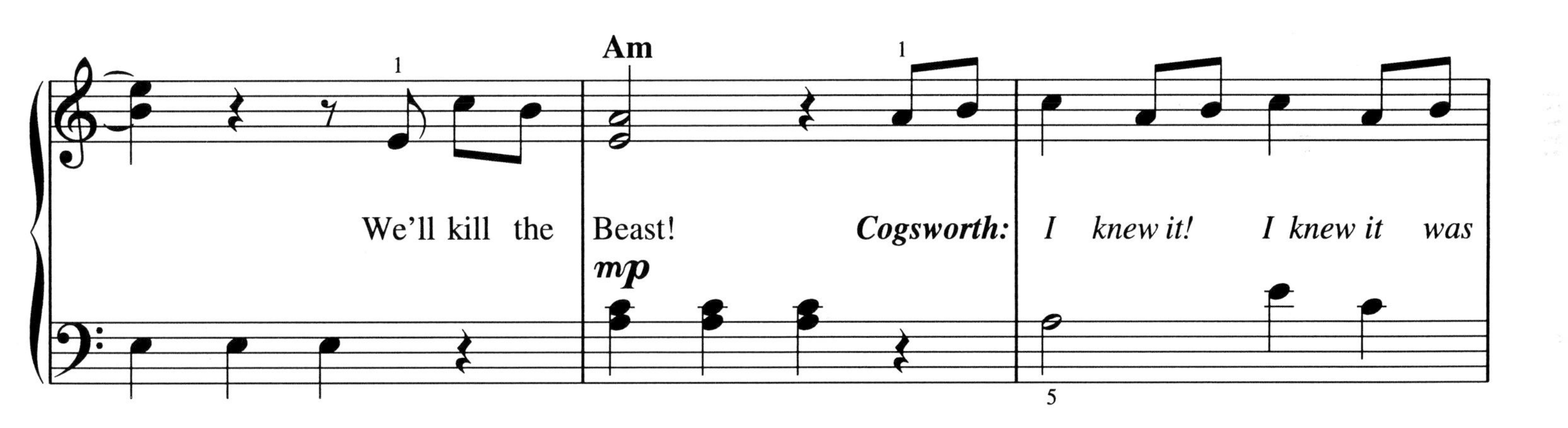
Am
We'll kill the
Beast!
Cogsworth:
I knew it! I knew it was
mp

foolish to get our hopes up.
Lumiere:
Maybe it would have been better if

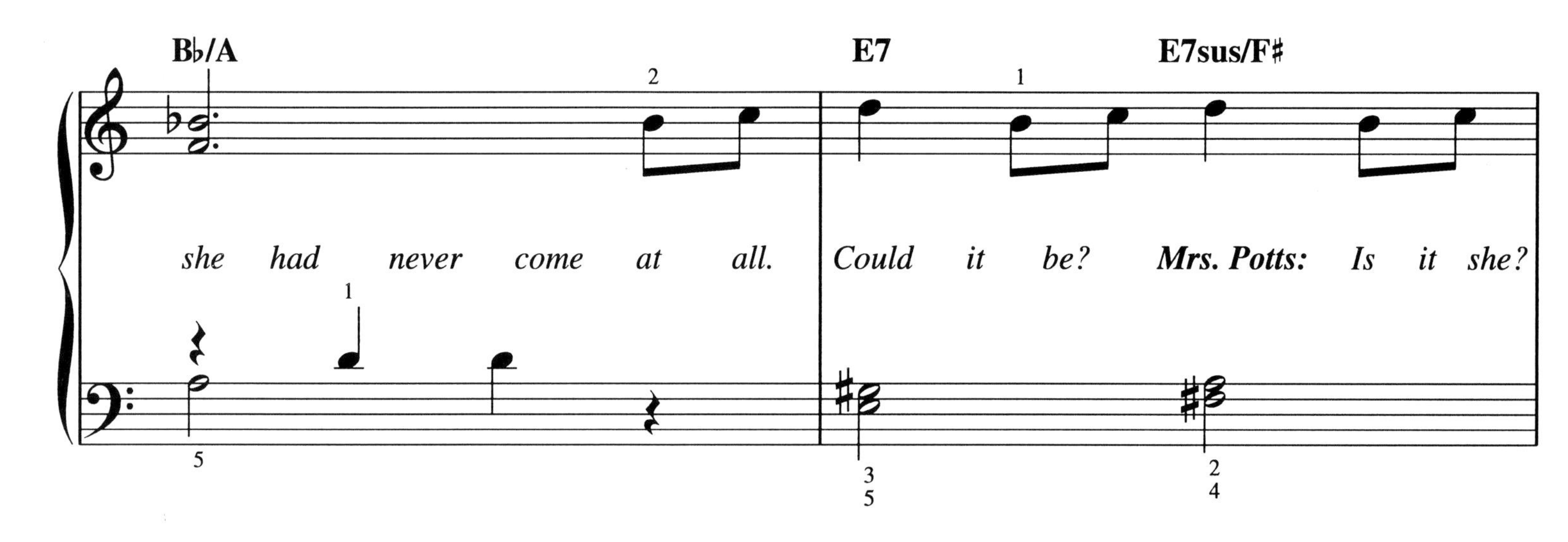
B♭/A
E7
E7sus/F♯
she had never come at all.
Could it be?
Mrs. Potts: Is it she?

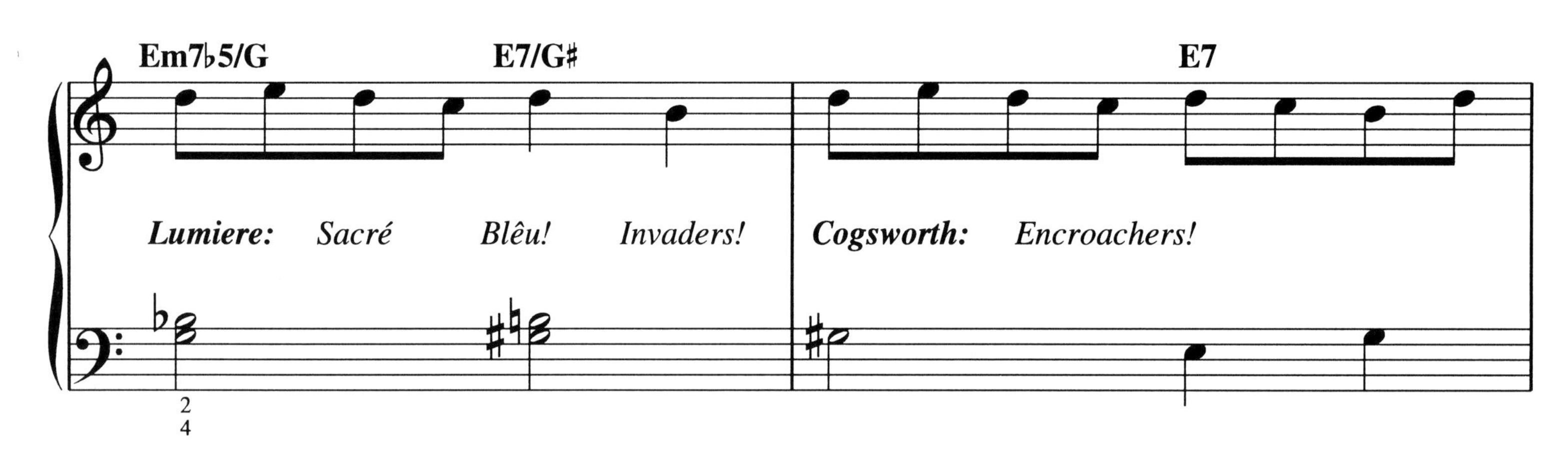
Em7♭5/G
E7/G♯
E7
Lumiere: Sacré Blêu! Invaders!
Cogsworth: Encroachers!

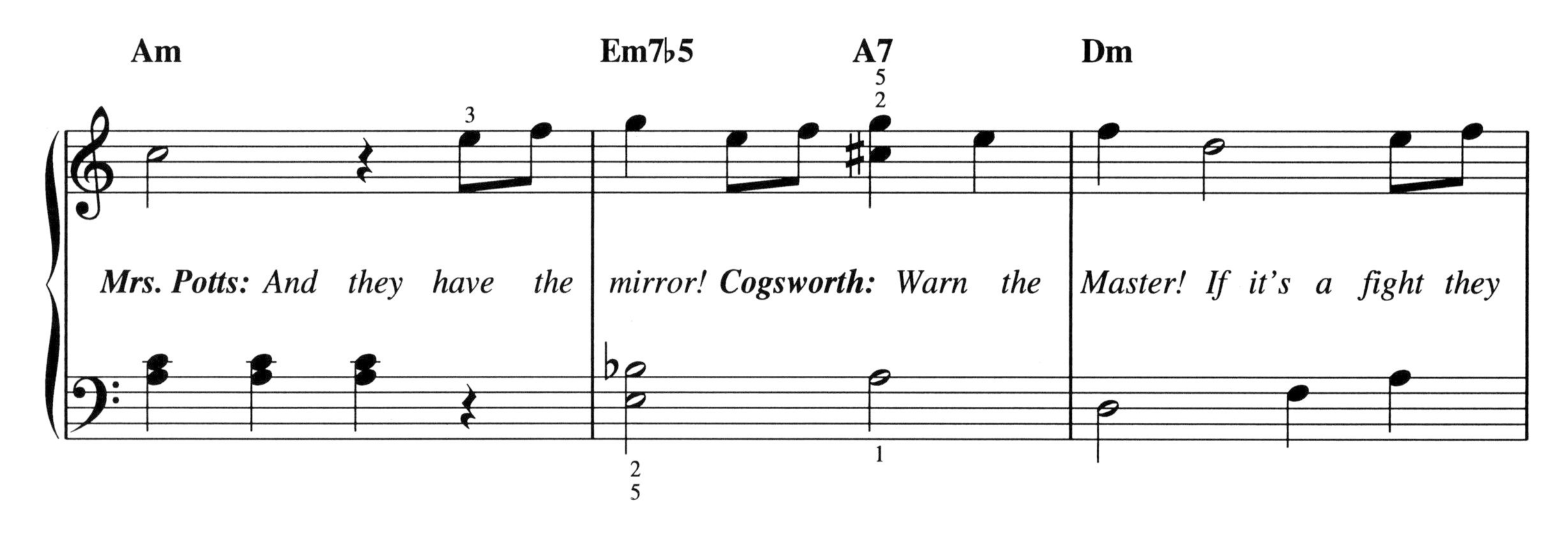
Am
Em7♭5
A7
Dm
Mrs. Potts: And they have the
mirror! Cogsworth: Warn the
Master! If it's a fight they

Em7♭5
A7
Dm
Bm7♭5
E7
want, we'll be ready for them!
Who's with me?
Gaston: Take whatever booty

E(no 3rd)
you can find. But remember,
the Beast is mine! Objects: Hearts a -
f

Am
blaze, ban - ners high, we go
march - ing in - to bat - tle un - a -

B♭/A
fraid, al - though the dan - ger just in -
creased. Mob: Raise the

E7
E7sus/F♯
Em7♭5/G
E7/G♯
flag! Sing the song! Here we
come we're fif - ty strong! And fif - ty

E7sus
French-men can't be wrong!
Let's kill the

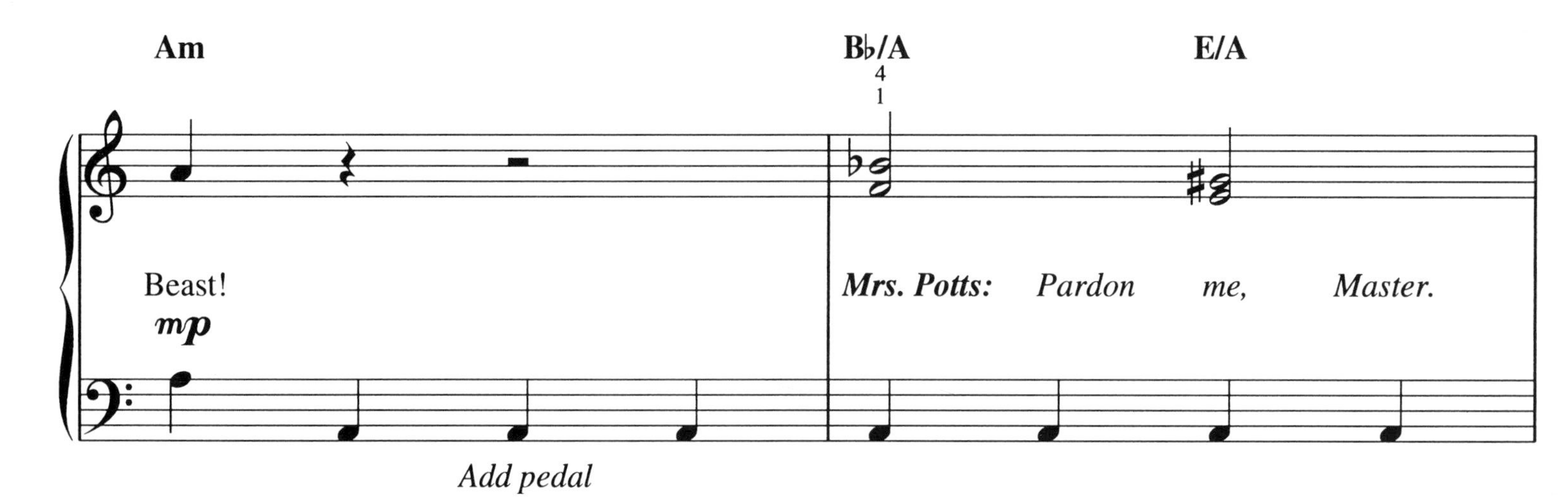
Am
B♭/A
E/A
Beast!
mp
Mrs. Potts: Pardon me, Master.
Add pedal

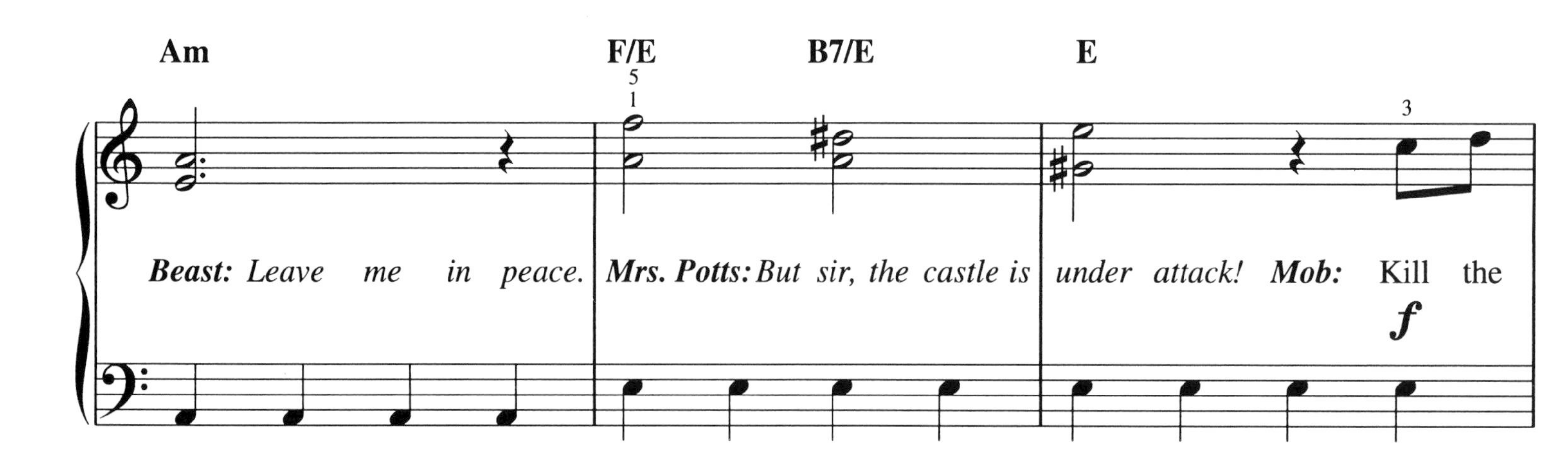
Am
F/E
B7/E
E
Beast: Leave me in peace.
Mrs. Potts: But sir, the castle is under attack!
Mob: Kill the
f

Esus
G♭/F
C7/F
Beast! Kill the Beast!
Lumiere: This isn't working!
mp

F
A♭/G
D7/G
G
Feather duster: Oh, Lumiere. We must do something! Lumiere: Wait, I know! Mob: Kill the
f

Gsus
A♭/G
D7/G
Beast! Kill the Beast! Mrs. Potts: What shall we do, Master?
mp

G
B♭/A
E7/A
A
Beast: It doesn't matter now. Just let them come. Mob: Kill the
ff
Stop pedal

Asus
Beast! Kill the Beast! Kill the Beast!

BEAUTY AND THE BEAST

Lyrics by HOWARD ASHMAN
Music by ALAN MENKEN

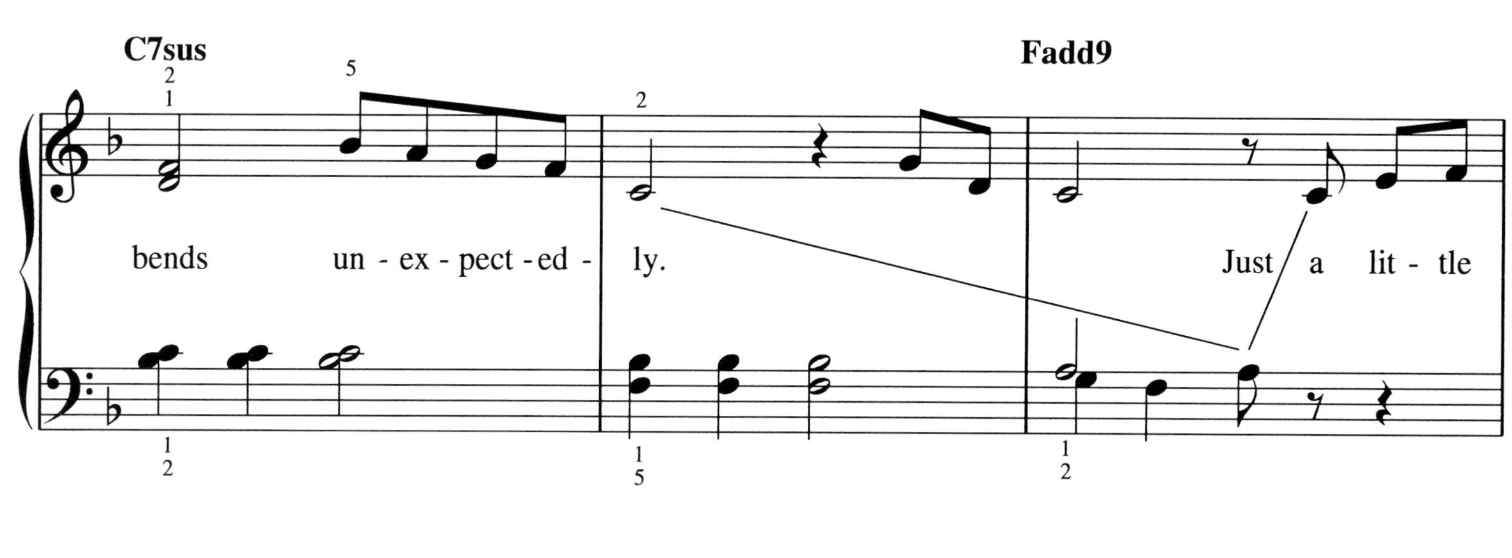
C7sus
Fadd9
bends un - ex - pect - ed - ly. Just a lit - tle

C7sus C Fadd9 Cm7 F7
change. Small, to say the least. Both a lit - tle

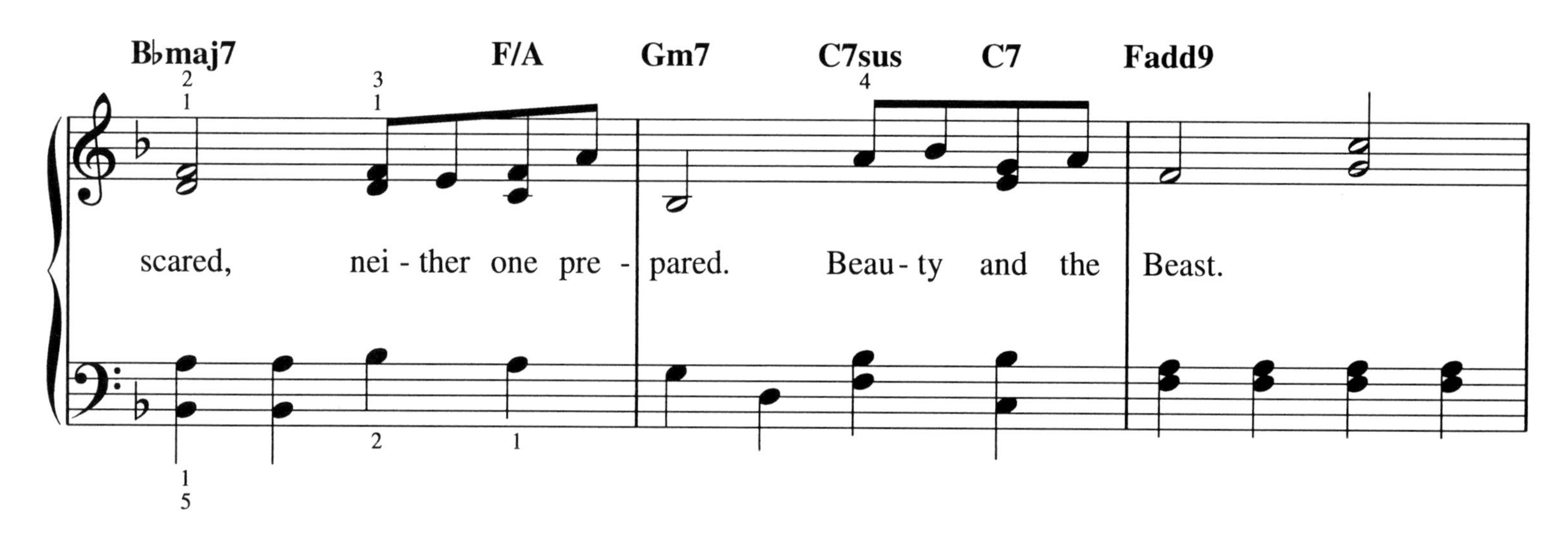
B♭maj7 F/A Gm7 C7sus C7 Fadd9
scared, nei - ther one pre - pared. Beau - ty and the Beast.

C7sus Am B♭add9
Ev - er just the same. Ev - er a sur -

Am
Bb add9
Am
prise.
mf
Ev - er as be - fore, ev - er just as
Dm7
Eb
G
C
sure as the sun will rise.
Tale as old as
G7sus
G
Cadd9
G7
time.
Tune as old as song.
Cadd9
Em
F
Bit - ter-sweet and strange, find - ing you can change, learn-ing you were

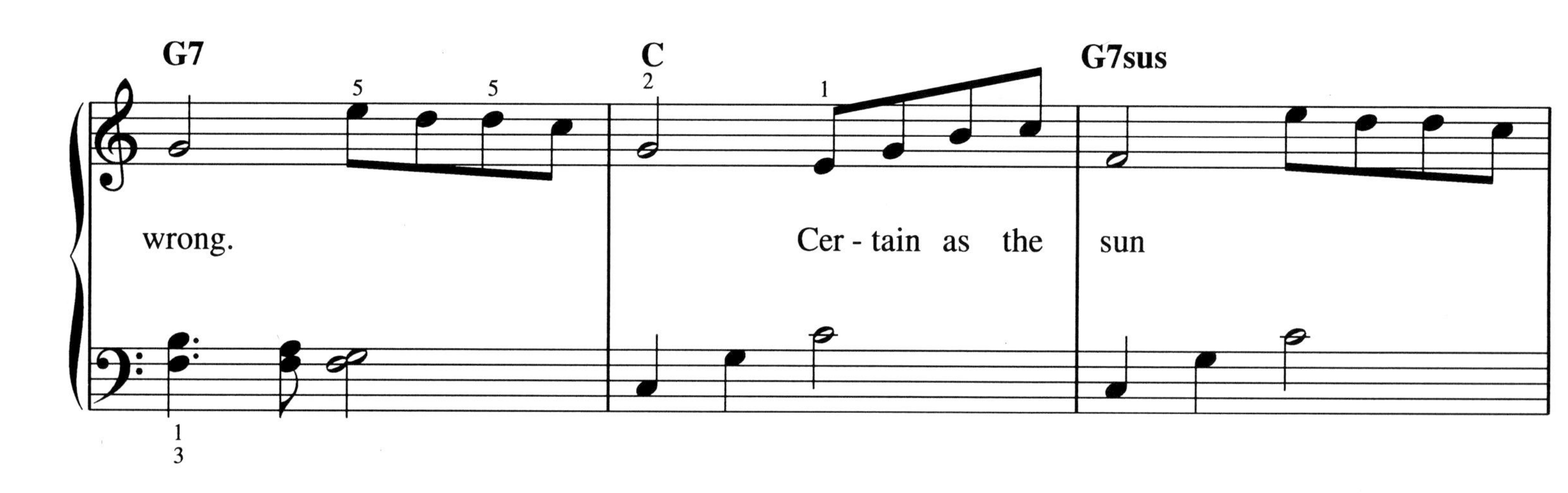
G7
C
G7sus
wrong.
Cer - tain as the
sun

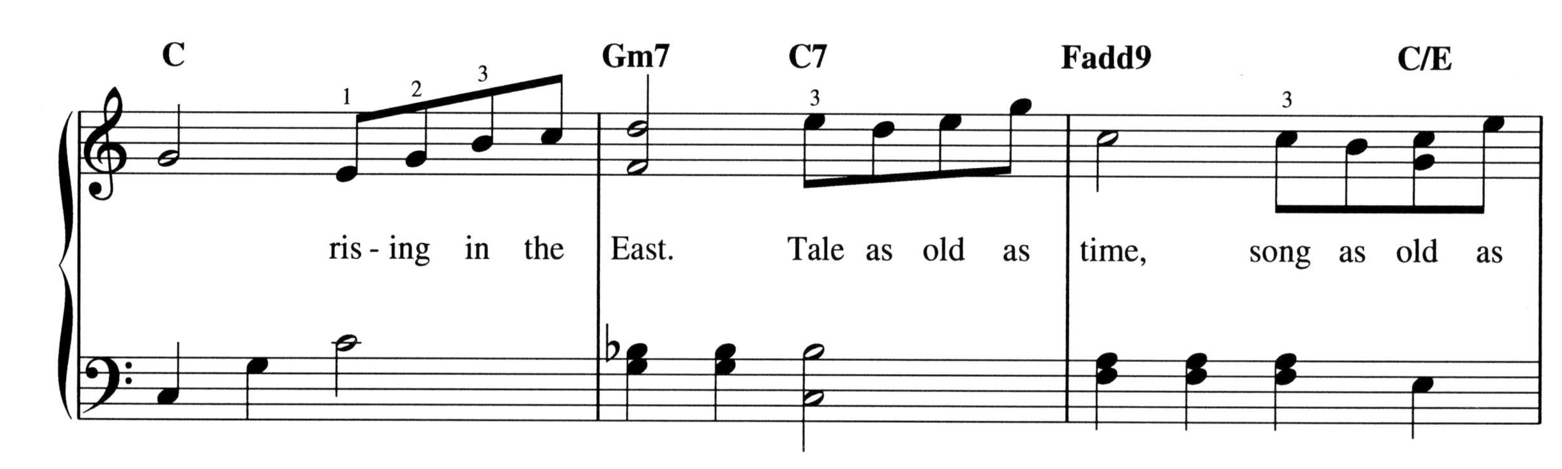
C
Gm7
C7
Fadd9
C/E
ris - ing in the
East.
Tale as old as
time,
song as old as

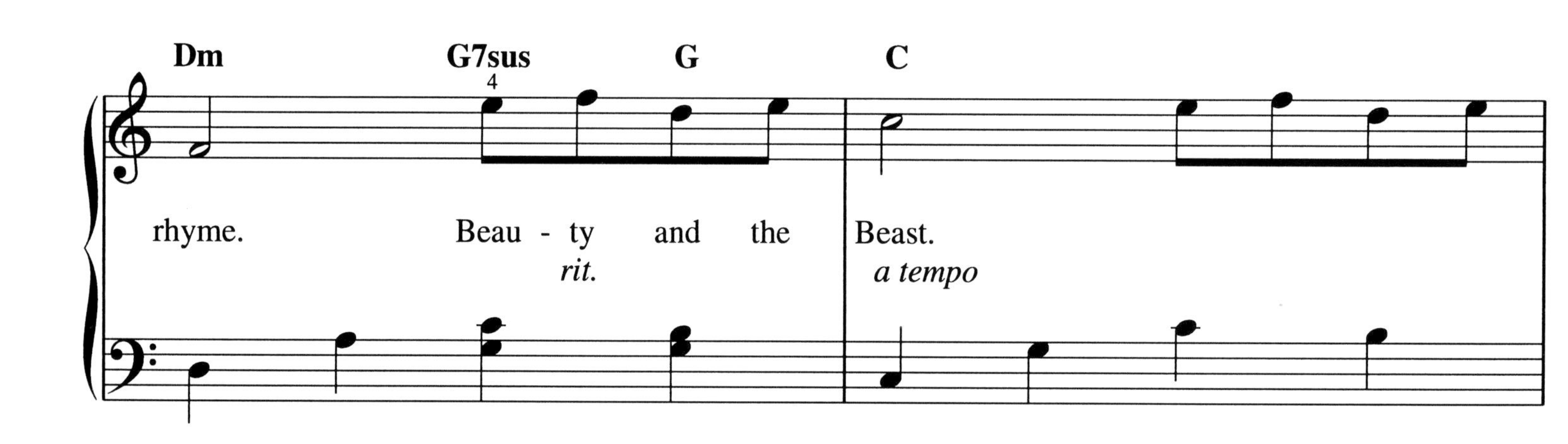
Dm
G7sus
G
C
rhyme.
Beau - ty and the
rit.
Beast.
a tempo

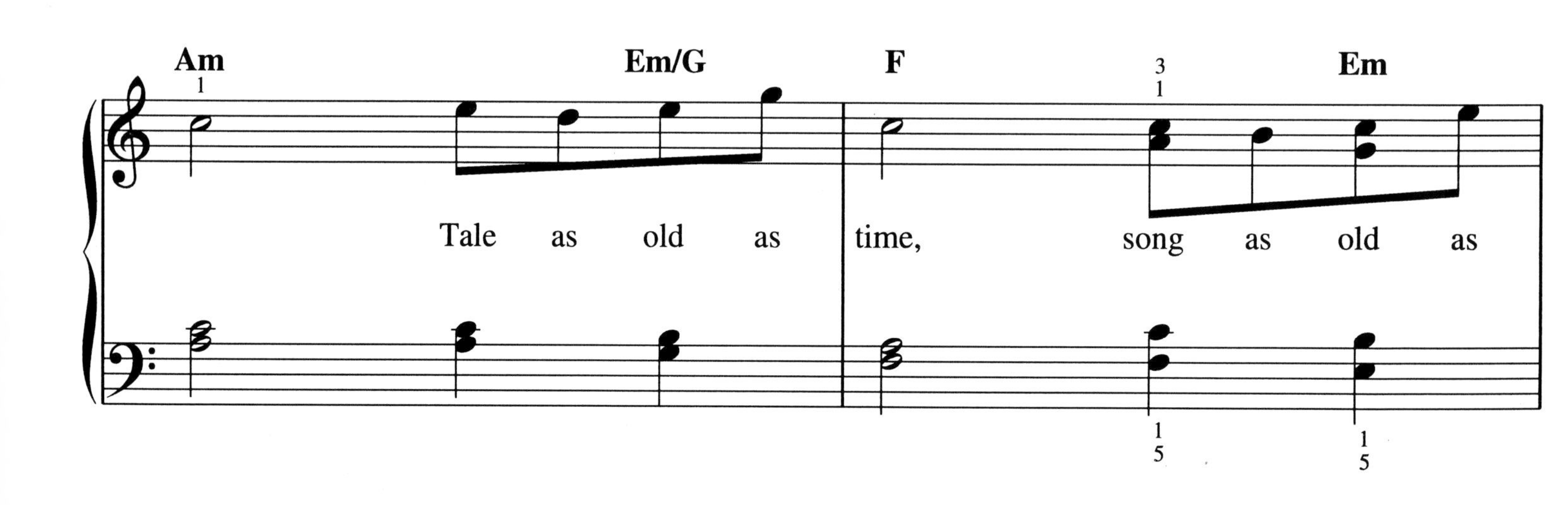
Am
Em/G
F
Em
Tale as old as
time,
song as old as

Dm
N.C.
Cadd9
rhyme.
Beau - ty
and
the
Beast.
a tempo
Csus
Cadd9
Csus
C
R.H.
L.H.
8va